THE

Inner Chamber and The Inner Life

THE

Inner Chamber and The Inner Life

BY

THE REV. ANDREW MURRAY, D.D.

KALPAZ

ISBN: 978-93-5128-850-3(PB)

First Published in 1905
Indian Reprint in 2017

Published by

Kalpaz Publications
C-30, Satyawati Nagar,
Delhi – 110052
E-mail: kalpaz@hotmail.com
Website: kalpazpublications.com
Ph.: +91-9212142040

PREFACE

THE Inner Chamber suggests thoughts of the utmost importance. The daily need of retirement and quiet; the true Spirit of prayer; the Devotional reading of God's Word; the Fellowship with God for which these are meant and by which alone they bring a blessing; the Spiritual Life which they are meant to strengthen and fit for daily duty in intercourse with the world; the Service for the Kingdom of God in Soul-winning and Intercession—all these truths have their share in making our devotions a source of joy and of strength. In this little book I have not attempted to take them up systematically, but I hope that the fragments I have given may bring help to some in the cultivation of the hidden life and its intercourse with God.

In this South African country there are various diseases that affect our orange trees. One of them is popularly known by the name of the root-disease. A tree may still be bearing, and an ordinary observer may not notice anything wrong, while an expert sees the beginning of a slow death. The phylloxera in the vineyards is nothing but a root-disease, and it has been found that there is no radical cure but by taking out the old roots and providing new ones. The old sort of grape is grafted on an American root, and in course of time you have the same stem and branches and fruit as before; BUT THE ROOTS ARE NEW and able to resist the disease. It is in the part of the plant that is HID FROM SIGHT, that the disease comes, and where healing must be sought.

How the Church of Christ, and the spiritual life of thousands of its members, suffers from the root-disease; the neglect of secret intercourse with God. It is the lack of secret prayer, the neglect of the maintenance of that hidden life "ROOTED in Christ," "ROOTED and grounded in love," that explains the feebleness of the Christian life to resist the world, and its failure to bring forth fruit abundantly. Nothing can change this but the restoration, in the life of the believer, of the inner chamber to the place which Christ meant it to have. As Christians learn, instead of trusting their own efforts, what it is daily to strike their roots deeper into Christ, and to make the secret personal fellowship with God their chief care, true godliness will flourish. "If the root be holy, so are the branches." If the morning hour be holy to the Lord, the day with its duties will be so too. If the root be healthy, so are the branches.

The most of these chapters have already appeared in *The South African Pioneer;* it is at the request of some who read them that I have consented to these now being republished. I pray that God may bless them to some of His children in the pursuit of the deeper and more fruitful life, the life hid with Christ in God.

ANDREW MURRAY.

CONTENTS

THE INNER CHAMBER

I

THE MORNING HOUR

"My voice shalt thou hear in the morning, O Lord; in the morning will I direct my prayer unto Thee, and will look up."—Ps. v. 3.

"The Lord God wakeneth morning by morning, He wakeneth mine ear to hear as they that are taught."—Is. l. 4.

FROM the earliest ages God's servants have thought of the morning as the time specially fitted for the worship of God. It is still regarded by all Christians both as a duty and a privilege to devote some portion of the beginning of the day to seeking retirement and fellowship with God. Many Christians, and specially the Student's Christian Association, observe The Morning Watch; the Y. P. C. E. Society speak of it as the Quiet Hour: others use the name of the Still Hour or the Quiet Time. All these, whether they think of a whole hour or half an hour, or a quarter of an hour, unite with the Psalmist in what he says, "My voice shalt thou hear in the morning, O Lord."

In speaking of the extreme importance of this daily time of quiet for prayer and meditation on God's Word, Mr. Mott has said:—

"Next to receiving Christ as Saviour, and claiming the Baptism of the Holy Spirit, we know of no act attended with larger good to ourselves or others, than the formation of an undiscourageable resolution to keep the morning watch, and spend the first half hour of the day alone with God." At first sight the statement appears too strong. The act of receiving Christ as Saviour is one of such infinite consequences for eternity, the act of claiming the Holy Spirit is one that works such a revolution in the Christian life, that such a simple thing as the firm determination to keep the morning watch hardly appears sufficiently important to be placed next to them. If, however, we think how impossible it is to live out our daily life in Christ as our Saviour from sin, or to maintain a walk in the leading and power of the Holy Spirit, without daily, close fellowship with God, we soon shall see the truth of the sentiment. Because it simply means the fixed determination that Christ shall have the whole life, that the Holy Spirit shall in everything be fully obeyed. The morning watch is the key to the position in which the surrender to Christ and the Holy Spirit can be unceasingly and fully maintained.

To realise this, let us look first at what ought to be THE OBJECT of the morning watch. The morning watch must not be regarded as an end in itself. It is not sufficient that it gives us a blessed time for prayer and Bible study, and so brings us a certain measure of refreshment and help. It is to serve as a means to an end. And that end is—to secure the presence of Christ for the whole day. Personal devotion to a friend or a pursuit means that that friend or pursuit shall always hold their place in the heart, even when other engagements occupy the attention. Personal devotion to Jesus means that we allow nothing to separate us from Him for a moment. To abide in Him and His love, to be kept by Him and His grace, to be doing His will and pleasing Him—this cannot possibly be an intermittent thing to one who is truly devoted to Him. "I need Thee every hour," "Moment by moment I am kept in His love." These hymns are the language of life and truth. "In Thy name shall they rejoice all the day," "I the Lord do keep it; I will water it every moment"—these are words of Divine power. The believer cannot stand for one moment without Christ. The personal devotion to Him refuses to be content with anything less than to abide always in His love and His will. Nothing less is the true scriptural Christian life. And the importance and blessedness and true aim of the morning watch can only be seen as nothing less than this is its first object.

The clearer the object of our pursuit is, the better we shall be able to adapt the means to its attainment. Consider the morning watch now as THE MEANS to this great end: I want to secure absolutely the presence of Christ all the day, to do nothing that can interfere with it. I feel at once that my success for the day will depend upon the clearness and the strength of the faith that seeks and finds and holds HIM in the closet. Meditation and prayer and the word will all be used as subordinate and auxiliary to this: the link for the day between Christ and me must be renewed and firmly fastened in the morning hour. At first it may appear as if the thought of the whole day, with all its possible cares, pleasures, temptations, may disturb the rest I have enjoyed in my quiet devotion. It is possible; but it will be no loss. True religion aims at having the character of Christ so formed in us, that in our most common acts His temper and disposition shall shew themselves. The spirit and the will of Christ are meant so to possess us that in our intercourse with men, in our relaxation, in our business, it shall be a second nature to us to act according to them. All this can be, because Christ Himself, as the Living One, lives in us. Be not disturbed if at first the aim appears too high or difficult, and occupies too much of your time in the hour of private prayer. The time you give it will be richly rewarded. You will return to prayer and scripture with new purpose and new faith. As the morning watch begins to have its effect on the day, the day will re-act on its first half hour, and fellowship with Christ have a new meaning and a new power.

It will specially have its influence on THE SPIRIT in which you keep the morning watch. As the grandeur of the aim—unbroken fellowship with God in Christ through the day—and the true nature of the means to secure it—a definite conscious meeting with Christ and a securing His presence for the day—possesses us, it will be seen that the one essential thing is, whole-hearted purpose: the fixed determination, whatever effort or self-denial it may cost, to win the prize. In study or on the sport field every student knows what need there is of vigorous will and determined purpose if we are to succeed. Religion needs, and indeed deserves, not less but more of intense devotion. If anything, surely the love of Christ needs the whole heart. It is this fixed determination before everything to secure Christ's presence, that will overcome every temptation to be unfaithful or superficial in the keeping of our pledges. It is this will make the morning watch itself a mighty means of grace in strengthening character, and nerving us to say No to every call for self-indulgence. It is this will enable us at once, when we enter the inner chamber and shut the door, to be there with our whole heart, ready at once for our intercourse with Christ. And it is this determination that, from the morning watch on, will become the keynote of our daily life.

In the world it is often said: Great things are possible to any man who knows what he wills, and wills it with all his heart. The student who has made personal devotion to Christ his watchword, will find in the morning hour the place where day by day the insight into his holy calling is renewed; where his will is braced up to walk worthy of it; and his faith rewarded by the presence of Christ waiting to meet him, and take charge of him for the day. We are more than conquerors through Him who loves us. A living Christ waits to meet us.

II

THE DOOR SHUT—ALONE WITH GOD

"When thou prayest enter into thine inner chamber, and, having shut thy door, pray to thy Father, which seeth in secret."—MATT. vi. 6.

MAN was created for fellowship with God. God made him in His own image and likeness, that he might be fit for this, capable of understanding and enjoying God, entering into His will and delighting in His glory. Because God is the Everywhere-present and All-pervading One, he could have lived in the enjoyment of an unbroken fellowship amidst whatever work he had to do.

Of this fellowship sin robbed us.

Nothing but this fellowship can satisfy the heart of either man or God. It was this Christ came to restore; to bring back to God His lost creature, and bring back man to all he was created for. Intercourse with God is the consummation of all blessedness on earth as in heaven. It comes when the promise, so often given, becomes a full experience: I will be with thee, I will never leave thee or forsake thee, and when we can say: The Father is always with me.

This intercourse with God is meant to be ours

all the day, whatever be our condition or the circumstances that surround us. But its enjoyment depends upon the reality of the intercourse in the inner chamber. The power of maintaining close and glad fellowship with God all the day will depend entirely upon the intensity with which we seek to secure it in the hour of secret prayer. The one essential thing in the Morning Watch or the Quiet Hour is—FELLOWSHIP WITH GOD.

It is this our Lord teaches is to be the inner secret of secret prayer: "Shut thy door, and pray to thy Father which seeth in secret." The first and chief thing is, see that there in secret you have the Father's Presence and Attention. Know that He sees and hears you. Of more importance than all your requests, however urgent, of more importance than all your earnestness and effort to pray aright, is this one thing—the childlike, living assurance that YOUR FATHER sees you, that you have now met Him, and that with His eye on you and yours on Him, you are now enjoying actual intercourse with Him.

Christian! there is a terrible danger to which you stand exposed in your inner chamber. You are in danger of substituting Prayer and Bible Study for living fellowship with God, the living interchange of giving Him your love, your heart, and your life, and receiving from Him His love, His life, and His spirit. Your needs and their expression, your desire to pray humbly and earnestly and believingly, may so occupy you, that the light of His countenance and the joy of His love cannot enter you. Your Bible Study may so interest you, and so waken pleasing religious sentiment, that—yes—the very Word of God may become a substitute for God Himself, THE GREATEST HINDRANCE TO FELLOWSHIP BECAUSE IT KEEPS THE SOUL OCCUPIED INSTEAD OF LEADING IT TO GOD HIMSELF. And we go out into the day's work without the power of an abiding fellowship, because in our morning devotions the blessing was not secured.

What a difference it would make in the life of many, if everything in the closet were subordinate to this one thing: I want through the day to walk with God; my morning hour is the time when my Father enters into a definite engagement with me and I with Him that it shall be so. What strength would be imparted by the consciousness: God has taken charge of me, He is going with me Himself; I am going to do His will all day in His strength; I am ready for all that may come. Yes, what a nobility would come into life, if secret prayer were not only an asking for some new sense of comfort, or light, or strength, but THE GIVING AWAY OF LIFE JUST FOR ONE DAY INTO THE SURE AND SAFE KEEPING OF A MIGHTY AND FAITHFUL GOD.

"Pray to thy Father which seeth in secret, and thy Father which seeth in secret will reward thee openly." Where the secret fellowship with the Father in spirit and in truth is maintained, the public life before men will carry the reward. The Father who sees in secret takes charge and rewards openly. Separation from men, in solitude with God—this is the sure, the only way to live in intercourse with men in the power of God's blessing.

III

THE OPEN DOOR—THE OPEN REWARD

"When thou fastest anoint thine head, and wash thy face that thou appear not unto men to fast, but to thy Father which seeth in secret, and thy Father which seeth in secret shall reward thee openly."—MATT. vi. 17.

"When they saw the boldness of Peter and John they took knowledge of them, that they had been with Jesus."—ACTS iv. 13.

"And it came to pass when Moses came down from Mount Sinai, that he wist not that the skin of his face shone while he talked with them. And when Aaron and all the children of Israel saw Moses, behold, the skin of his face shone; and they were afraid to come nigh to him. And till Moses had done speaking with them, he put a veil upon his face."—EXOD. xxxiv. 29-33.

THE transition from the fellowship with God in the morning hour to the intercourse with our fellowmen is often difficult. If we have met God, we long to maintain the sense of His presence, and our surrender to Him. We go out to the breakfast table, where, perhaps in the bosom of our own family, the atmosphere is all at once changed, and as the presence of men and the visible asserts itself, we begin to lose what we had found. Many a young Christian has been perplexed with the question how to keep his heart filled with that of which he does not feel at liberty, or has not the opportunity, to speak. Even in religious circles it is not always easy to have free intercourse, through lack of fervour or boldness, on that which would give the greatest profit and pleasure. Let us strive to learn how our intercourse with men, may be, instead of a hindrance, a help to the maintenance of a life of continual fellowship with God.

The lessons which the story of Moses with the veil on his face teach, are very suggestive. Close and continued fellowship with God will in due time leave its mark and make itself manifest before men. Moses wist not that his face shone: the light of God shining from us will be unconscious; it will but deepen the sense of our being an earthen vessel (1 Cor. ii. 3, 4, and 2 Cor. iv.). The sense of God's presence in a man may often cause others to fear, or at least to feel ill at ease in, his company. When others observe what is to be seen in him, the true believer will know what it is to veil his face, and prove by humility and love that he is indeed a man of like passions with those around him. And yet, through all, there will be the proof, too, that he is a man of God, who lives in, and has dealings with, an unseen world.

The same lessons are taught by what our Lord says about fasting. Make no show of thy fasting, so that thou appear not unto men to fast; meet them in the joy and kindness of God's gentleness, as the Father's beloved and loving child. COUNT UPON GOD, WHO HAS SEEN THEE IN SECRET, TO REWARD THEE OPENLY, TO GIVE THEE GRACE IN INTERCOURSE WITH HIM, AND TO MAKE THEM KNOW THAT HIS GRACE AND LIGHT ARE ON THEE.

The story of Peter and John confirms the same truth: they had been with Jesus not only while He was on earth, but as He entered into the heavenlies, and had received His spirit. They simply acted out what the spirit of Christ taught them; even enemies could see by their boldness that they had been with Jesus.

The blessing of intercourse with God may easily be lost by entering too deeply into intercourse with men. The spirit of the inner chamber must be carried out into a holy watchfulness throughout the day. We know not at what hour the enemy may come. This continuance of the morning watch may be maintained by a quiet self-restraint, in not giving the reins to nature. It has, in a religious home circle, often sought help, in each one repeating a text at the breakfast table on some fixed subject, giving easy occasion to religious conversation. When once the abiding sense of God's presence and of intercourse with Him—"be thou in the fear of God all the day long"—has become the aim of the morning hour, with the deepest humility and the most loving intercourse with those around us, grace will be sought and found to pass on into the day's duties with the continuity of fellowship kept unbroken. It is a great thing to enter the inner chamber, and shut to the door, and meet the Father in secret. It is a greater thing to open the door again, and go out, in an enjoyment of that Presence which nothing can disturb.

To some, such a life does not appear needful; the strain is too great; one can be a good Christian without it. To those who seek to be men of one thing, who feel that if they are to be true and mighty to influence the church and the world around them they must be full of God and His Presence, everything will be subordinate to the one question: How to bear in the earthen vessel the heavenly treasure, the power of Christ resting on us all the day.

IV

MOSES AND THE WORD OF GOD

IN regard to the connection between prayer and the word in our private devotion, the expression of a convert from heathenism has often been quoted: I pray, I speak to God; I read in the Bible, God speaks to me. There is a verse in the history of Moses, in which this thought is beautifully brought out. We read, Numbers vii, 89, "WHEN MOSES WAS GONE INTO THE TABERNACLE TO SPEAK WITH GOD, THEN HE HEARD THE VOICE OF ONE SPEAKING TO HIM FROM OFF THE MERCY SEAT: AND GOD SPAKE UNTO HIM." When he went in to pray for himself or his people, and to wait for instructions, he found One waiting for him. What a lesson for our morning watch. A prayerful spirit is the spirit to which God will speak. A prayerful spirit will be a listening spirit waiting to hear what God says. In the intercourse with God His presence and the part He takes must be as real as my own. We want to ask what is needed that our Scripture reading and praying may be such true fellowship with God.

First, GET INTO THE RIGHT PLACE. "Moses went into the tabernacle to speak with God." He separated himself from the people, and went where he could be with God alone. He went to the place where God was to be found. Jesus has told us where that place is. He calls us to enter into our closet, and shut the door, and pray to our Father which seeth in secret. Anywhere where we really are ALONE WITH GOD may be to us the secret of His presence. To speak with God needs separation from all else. It needs a heart intently set upon and in full expectation of meeting God personally, and having direct dealings with Him. Those who go there to speak to **God**, will hear the Voice of One speaking to them.

Next, GET INTO THE RIGHT POSITION. He heard the Voice of One speaking from off the mercy seat. Bow before the mercy seat. THERE the consciousness of your unworthiness will not hinder you, but be a real help in trusting God. THERE you may have the assured confidence that your upward look will be met by His eye, that your prayer can be heard, that His loving answer will be given. Bow before the mercy seat, and be sure that the God of Mercy will see and bless you.

And then, GET INTO THE RIGHT DISPOSITION—the listening attitude. Many are so occupied with the much or the little they have to say in their prayers, that the Voice of One speaking off the mercy seat is never heard, because it is not expected or waited for. "Thus saith the Lord, The heaven is My throne, and the earth is My footstool; to this man will I look, even to him that is POOR AND OF A CONTRITE SPIRIT, AND TREMBLETH AT MY WORD." Let us enter the closet, and set ourselves to pray, with a heart that humbly waits to hear God speak; in the Word we read; we shall indeed hear the Voice of One speaking to us. The highest blessedness of prayer will be our ceasing to pray, to let God speak.

Prayer and the Word are inseparably linked together: power in the use of either depends upon the presence of the other. The Word gives me matter for prayer, telling me what God will do for me. It shows me the path of prayer, telling me how God would have me come. It gives me the power for prayer, the courage of the assurance I will be heard. And it brings me the answer to prayer, as it teaches what God will do for me. And so, on the other hand, prayer prepares the heart for receiving the Word from God Himself, for the teaching of the Spirit to give the spiritual understanding of it, for the faith that is made partaker of its mighty working.

It is clear why this is so. Prayer and the Word have one common centre—God. Prayer seeks God: the Word reveals God. In prayer man asks God: in the Word God answers man. In prayer man rises to heaven to dwell with God: in the Word God comes to dwell with man. In prayer man gives himself to God: in the Word God gives Himself to man.

In prayer and the Word it must be all—God.

Make God the all of thy heart, the one object of thy desire; prayer and the Word will be a blessed fellowship with God, the interchange of thought, and love and life: a dwelling in God and God in us. Seek God and live!

V

MOSES, THE MAN OF PRAYER

BEFORE Moses was the patriarchal dispensation, with the family life, and the power the fathers had, marking it. Moses is the first man appointed to be a teacher and leader of men. In him we find wonderful illustrations of the place and power of intercession in the servant of God.

Moses' Prayers.—In Egypt, from his first call, Moses prayed. He asked God what he was to say to the people, Exod. iii. 11-13. He told Him all his weakness, and besought Him to be relieved of his mission, iv. 1-13. When the people reproached him that their burdens were increased, he went and told God, v. 22, and he made known to Him all his fears, vi. 12. This was his first training. Out of this was born his power in prayer when, time after time, Pharaoh asked him to entreat the Lord for him, and deliverance came at Moses' request (viii. 8, 9, 12, 28, 29, 30, 31; ix. 28, 29, 33; x. 17, 18). Study these passages until you come under the full impression of how real a factor in Moses' work and God's redemption prayer was.

At the Red Sea, Moses cried to God with the people and the answer came (xiv. 15). In the wilderness when the people thirsted, and when

Amalek attacked them, it was also prayer that brought deliverance (xvii. 4, 11).

At Sinai, when Israel had made the Golden Calf, it was prayer that at once averted the threatened destruction, xxxii. 11, 14. It was renewed prayer that gained them restoration, xxxii. 31. It was more prayer that secured God's presence to go with them (xxxiii. 17), and once again it was prayer that brought the revelation of God's glory (xxxiii. 19). And when that had been given it was fresh prayer that received the renewal of the covenant, xxxiv. 9, 10.

In Deuteronomy we have a wonderful summary of all this, ix. 18, 19, 20, 26; we see with what intensity he prayed, and how in one case it was for forty days and forty nights that he fell on his face before the Lord, ix. 25; x. 10.

In Numbers we read of Moses' prayer quenching the fire of the Lord, xi. 2, and obtaining the supply of meat; xi. 2, 11, of prayer healing Miriam, xii. 13; of prayer again saving the nation when they had refused to go up to the land, xiv. 17-20. Prayer brought down judgment on Korah, xvi. 15, and when God would consume the whole congregation, prayer made atonement, 46. Prayer brought water out of the rock, xx. 6, and in answer to prayer the brazen serpent was given, xxi. 7. To prayer God's will was made known in a case of difficulty, xxvii. 5, and Joshua given as Moses' successor, 16.

Study all this until your whole heart is filled

with the thought of the part prayer must play, may play, in the life of a man who would be God's servant to his fellowmen.

As we study, the parts will unite into a living whole and Moses will be to us a living model for our prayer life. We shall learn what is needed to be an intercessor. The lessons that will come to us will be such as these:—

I see Moses was a man given up to God, zealous, yea, jealous for God, for His honour and will.

A man, too, absolutely given up to his people, ready to sacrifice himself, if they may be saved.

A man conscious of a Divine calling to act as mediator, to be the link, the channel of communication and of blessing, between a God in heaven and men on earth. A life so entirely possessed by this mediatorial consciousness that nothing can be more simple and natural than to expect that God will hear.

I see here God in answer to the prayers of one man saves and blesses those He has entrusted to him, and does what He would not do without it. I see how the whole government of God has taken up prayer into its plan as one of its constituent parts. I see how heaven is filled with the life and power and blessing earth needs, and how the prayer of earth is the power to bring that blessing down.

I see above all how prayer is an index of the spiritual life, and how its power depends upon my relation to God, and the consciousness of being

His representative. He entrusts His work to me, and the more simple and entire my devotion to His interests are, the more natural and certain becomes the assurance that He hears me.

Think of the place God had in Moses' life, as the God who had sent him, the God to whom he was wholly devoted, the God who had promised to be with him, and who would and did always help him when and as he prayed.

Now for the practical application: How to learn to pray like Moses? We cannot secure this grace by an act of the will. Our first lesson must be, the sense of impotence. Then grace will work it in us, slowly and surely, if we give ourselves into its training. But though the training will be gradual, there is one thing can be done at once, we can AT ONCE decide to give ourselves to this life and take up the right position. Do this now, take the decision, TO LIVE ENTIRELY TO BE A CHANNEL FOR GOD'S BLESSING TO FLOW THROUGH YOU TO THE WORLD. TAKE THE STEP. If need be, take ten minutes for deliberate thought. Accept the Divine appointment, and take up some object of intercession.

Take time, say a week, and get firm hold of the elementary truths Moses' example teaches. As a music teacher insists upon practising the scales—only practice makes perfect—set yourself to learn thoroughly and to apply the needed first lessons.

God seeks men through whom He can bless the world. Say definitely, Here am I: I will give my life to this. Cultivate large faith in the simple truth: God hears prayer; God will do what I ask.

Give yourself as wholly to men as to God, and set your eyes open to a sense of the need of a perishing world. Take up your position in Christ, and in the power which His Name, and Life and Spirit give you. And go on practising definite intercession.

VI

MOSES, THE MAN OF GOD

"Moses, the man of God, blessed the children of Israel."—DEUT. xxxiii. 1

THE man of God! How much the name means! A man who comes from God, chosen and sent of Him. A man who walks with God, lives in His fellowship and carries the mark of His presence. A man who lives for God and His will; whose whole being is pervaded and ruled by the glory of God; who involuntarily and unceasingly leads men to think of God. A man in whose heart and life God has taken the right place as the All in All, and who has only one desire, that He should have that place throughout the world.

Such men of God are what the world needs; such are what God seeks, that He may fill them with Himself, and send them into the world to help others to know Him. Such a man Moses was so distinctly that men naturally spoke of him thus—Moses, the man of God! Such a man every servant of God ought to aim at being—a living witness and proof of what God is to him in heaven, and is to him on earth, and what He claims to be in all.

In a previous chapter we spoke of Intercourse with God as what man had been created for, as the privilege of daily life, as what was to be our first care in the morning watch. What was there said had chiefly reference to our personal need, and the power of a godly happy life influencing others. The name, Moses, the man of God! and the thought of a man being so closely and manifestly linked to God that men as by instinct gave this as his chief characteristic—the man of God! —leads us farther. It brings us out into public life, it suggests the idea of the impression we make upon men, and the power we can have of so carrying the sign of God's holy presence with us that when men see us or think of us, the name shall at once suggest itself—THE MAN OF GOD.

These are the men the world and God equally need. And why? Because the world, by sin, has fallen away from God. Because in Christ the world has been redeemed for God. And because God has no way of showing men what they ought to be, of awakening and calling and helping them, but through men of God, in whom His life, His spirit, His power are working. Man was created for God, that God might live and dwell and work and show forth His glory in him and through him. God was to be his all in all. The indwelling of God was to be as natural and delightful as it is true, strange and incomprehensible. When the redemption of Christ was completed in the descent of God the Holy Spirit into the hearts of men, this indwelling was restored, God regained possession of His home. And where a man GIVES

HIMSELF UP WHOLLY TO THE PRESENCE OF THE HOLY SPIRIT, not only as a power working in him, but AS GOD DWELLING IN HIM (John xiv. 16, 20, 23; 1 John iv.) he may become, in the deepest meaning of the word, A MAN OF GOD!

Paul tells us that it is through the power of Holy Scripture that "the man of God is complete." This suggests that with some the life is imperfect, and needs to be made perfect. "Every scripture is inspired of God, and is profitable for teaching, for reproof, for correction, for instruction in righteousness, that THE MAN OF GOD MAY BE COMPLETE, furnished completely to every good work." This brings us again to the morning watch as the chief time for personal Bible study. It is as we yield heart and life to the Word, for God through its teaching, its reproof, its correction, its instruction to search and form our whole life, and be thus come under the direct operation of God, and into full intercourse with Him, that THE MAN OF GOD WILL BE COMPLETE—furnished to every good work.

Oh! for grace to be truly a man of God! A man that knows and proves these three things; God is all; God claims all; God works all. A man that has seen the place God has in His universe and in men—He is THE ALL IN ALL! A man who has understood that God ASKS AND MUST HAVE ALL, and who only lives to give God His due and His glory! A man who has discovered the great secret that GOD WORKS ALL, and seeks, like the Son of God, to live in the unceasing blessed dependence that the Father in Him speaks the words and does the work.

Brother! seek to be a man of God! Let God in the morning watch be all to thee. Let God during the day be all to thee. And let thy life be devoted to one thing, to bring men to God, and God to men, so that in His Church, and in the world, God may have the place due to Him.

"If I be a man of God, let fire come down from heaven." Thus answered Elijah when the captain called him to come down. The true God is the God who answers by fire. And the true man of God is he who knows how to call down the fire, because he has power with the God of heaven. Whether the fire be that of judgment or the Holy Spirit, the work of the man of God is to bring fire down to earth. What the world needs is the man of God who knows God's power, and his power with God.

Do believe that it is in the secret prayer habit of daily life that we learn to know our God, and His fire, and our power with Him. Oh! to know what it is to be a man of God, and what it implies.

In Elijah as in Moses we see how it just means a separation from every other interest, an entire identification with the honour of God, no longer a man of the world, but A MAN OF GOD.

There is a secret feeling that all this brings more strain and sacrifice, difficulty and danger, than we are ready for. This is only true as long as we have not seen how absolute God's claim is, how unutterably blessed it is to yield to it, and how certain that God Himself will work it in us.

Turn back now and look at Moses, the man of prayer, Moses, the man of the word, and see how out of these three grew—Moses, the man of God. See the same in the life of Elijah—the harmony between our hearing God's word and His hearing ours, and the way in which it becomes Divinely possible to be and live—A MAN OF GOD. And study then the application.

VII

THE POWER OF GOD'S WORD

"The word of God which worketh in you that believe."—1 THESS. ii. 12.

THE value of the words of a man depends upon my knowledge of him who speaks. What a difference when a man gives me the promise, I will give you the half of all I have, whether the speaker be a poor man who owns a shilling, or a millionaire who offers to share his fortune with me. One of the first requisites to fruitful Bible study is the knowledge of God as the Omnipotent One, and of the power of His word.

The power of God's word is infinite. "By the word of the Lord were the heavens made. He spake and it was done; He commanded and it stood fast." In the word of God His omnipotence works: it has creative power and calls into existence THE VERY THING OF WHICH IT SPEAKS.

As the word of the Living God it is a living word, and gives life. It can not only call into existence, but even make alive again that which is dead. Its quickening power can raise dead bodies, can give eternal life to dead souls. All spiritual life comes through it, for we are born of incorruptible seed by the word of God that liveth and abideth for ever.

Here there lies, hidden from many, one of the deepest secrets of the blessing of God's word—the faith in its creative and quickening energy. THE WORD WILL WORK IN ME THE VERY DISPOSITION OR GRACE WHICH IT COMMANDS OR PROMISES. "It worketh effectually in them that believe." Nothing can resist its power when received into the heart through the Holy Spirit "It worketh effectually in them that believe." "The voice of the Lord is in power." Everything depends upon learning the art of receiving that word into the heart. And in learning this art the first step is—FAITH IN ITS LIVING, ITS OMNIPOTENT, ITS CREATIVE POWER. By His word "God calleth the things that are not, as though they were."

As true as this is of all God's mighty deeds from creation on to the resurrection of the dead, it is true too of every word spoken to us in His holy book. Two things keep us from believing this as we should. The one is the terrible experience in all around, and perhaps in ourselves too, of the word being made of none effect by human wisdom or unbelief or worldliness. The other the neglect of the teaching of Scripture that the word is a seed. Seeds are small, seeds may be long dormant, seeds have to be hidden, and when they sprout are of slow growth. Because the action of God's word is hidden and unobserved, slow and apparently feeble, we do not believe in its omnipotence. Let us make it one of our first lessons. The word I study is the power of God unto salvation: IT

WILL WORK IN ME IN ALL I NEED, ALL THE FATHER ASKS.

What a prospect this faith would open up for our spiritual life! We should see all the treasures and blessings of God's grace to be within our reach. The word has power to enlighten our darkness: in our hearts it will bring the light of God, the sense of His love, and the knowledge of His will. The word can fill us with strength and courage to conquer every enemy, and to do whatever God asks us to do. The word would cleanse, and sanctify, would work in us faith and obedience, would become in us the seed of every trait in the likeness of our Lord. Through the word the Spirit would lead us into all truth, that is, make all that is in the word true in us, and so prepare our heart to be the habitation of the Father and the Son.

What a change would come over our relation to God's word and to the Morning watch if we really believed this simple truth. Let us begin our training for that ministry of the word which every believer must exercise, by proving its power in our own experience. Let us begin to seek this, quietly setting ourselves to learn the great faith-lesson, the mighty power of God's word. Nothing less than this is meant by saying: THE WORD OF GOD IS TRUE! because God himself will make it true in us. We shall have much to learn in regard to what hinders that power, much to overcome to be freed from these hindrances, much to surrender to receive that working. But all will come right if we will only set out upon our Bible study with the determined resolve to believe that GOD'S WORD HAS OMNIPOTENT POWER IN THE HEART TO WORK EVERY BLESSING OF WHICH IT SPEAKS.

VIII

THE SEED IS THE WORD

I THINK it may be confidently said that in all nature there is no other illustration of what the Word of God is, so true, so full of meaning, as that of the seed. To have a full spiritual insight into it is a wonderful means of grace.

The points of resemblance are easily stated. There is the apparent insignificance of the seed—a little thing as compared with the tree that springs from it. There is the life, enclosed and dormant within a husk. There is the need of a suitable soil, without which growth is impossible. There is the slow growth with its length of time calling for the long patience of the husbandman. And there is the fruit, in which the seed reproduces and multiplies itself. In all these respects, the seed teaches us most precious lessons as to our use of God's Word.

There is first THE LESSON OF FAITH. Faith does not look at appearances. As far as we can judge, it looks most improbable that a Word of God should give life in the soul, should work in us the very grace of which it speaks, should transform our whole character, should fill us with strength. And yet so it is. When once we have learned to believe that the Word can work effectually the very truth of which it is the expression; we have found one of the chief secrets of our Bible Study. We shall then receive each word as the pledge and the power of a Divine working.

Then there is THE LESSON OF LABOUR. The seed needs to be gathered, and kept, and put into the prepared soil. And so the mind has to gather from scripture and understand and pass on to the heart, as the only soil on which this heavenly seed can grow, the words which meet our need. We cannot give the life or the growth. Nor do we need to: it is there. But what we can do is to hide the Word in our heart, and keep it there, waiting for the sunshine that comes from above.

And the seed teaches THE LESSON OF PATIENCE. The effect of the Word on the heart is in most cases not immediate. It needs time to strike root, and grow up: Christ's words must abide in us. We must not only day by day increase our store of Bible knowledge—this is only like gathering the grain in a barn—but watch over those words of command or promise that we have specially taken, and allow them room in our heart to spread both root and branches. We need to know what seed we have put in, and to cultivate a watchful but patient expectancy. In due time we shall reap, if we faint not.

And last comes THE LESSON OF FRUITFULNESS. However insignificant that little seed of a Word of God appears, however feeble its life may seem, however deep hidden the very thought of what it speaks may be, and however trying the slowness of its growth may be to our patience—be sure the fruit will come. The very truth and life and power of God, of which the Word contained the thought, will grow and ripen within you. And just as a seed bears a fruit, containing the same seed for new reproduction, so the Word will not only bring you the fruit it promised, but that fruit will each time become a seed which you carry to others to give life and blessing.

Not only the Word, but "the kingdom of heaven is like a seed." And all the grace of it comes in no other way than as a hidden seed in the heart of the regenerate. Christ is a seed. The Holy Spirit is a seed. The love of God shed abroad in the heart is a seed. The exceeding greatness of the power that worketh in us is a seed. The hidden life is there in the heart, but not at once or always felt in its power. The Divine glory is there, but often without form or comeliness, to be known only by faith, to be counted and acted on even when not felt, to be waited for in its springing forth and its growth.

As this central truth each time is firmly grasped and held as the law of all the heavenly life on earth, the study of God's word becomes an act of faith and surrender and dependence upon the living God. I believe humbly, almost tremblingly, in the Divine seed that there is in the Word, and the power of God's Spirit to make it true in my life and experience. I yield my heart hungrily and wholly to receive this Divine seed. And I wait on God in absolute dependence and confidence to give the increase in a power above what we can ask or think.

IX

DOING AND KNOWING

"But Jesus said, 'Yea rather, blessed are they that hear the word of God, *and keep it.*'"—LUKE ii. 28.

"If any man willeth *to do* His will, he shall *know.*" —JOHN vii. 17.

SOME time ago I received a letter from one who was evidently an earnest Christian, asking me for some hints to help him in Bible study. My first thought was to answer that there are so many addresses and booklets on the subject, that he would find all I could say, better said already. After a little while, certain experiences in my own immediate circle made me feel how needful instruction was on this all-important subject, and I found there were points to which it appeared desirable that special prominence should be given. I take up my pen with the earnest prayer and hope that what I write may be from God, the fountain of Light and Life, to help His young children to see how they may draw from His precious Word all that Divine instruction and nourishment, all that abundant joy and strength which He has there laid up for them.

I suppose myself addressing a young Christian who has said to me,—Help me to study my Bible.

Give me some rules to guide me as to how to begin, and how to go on, so that I may know my Bible well. The very first thing I have to. say to him, the thing that comes before all else, is this:— In your Bible study everything will depend upon the spirit in which you come to it, upon the Object or End you propose to yourself. In worldly things a man is ruled and urged on by the End or Aim he sets before himself. It is not otherwise with the Bible. If your aim be simply to know the Bible well, you will be disappointed. If you think that the thorough knowledge of the Bible will necessarily be a blessing, you are mistaken. To some it is a curse. To others it is powerless, it does not make them either holy or happy. To some it is a burden, it depresses them instead of quickening them or lifting them up.

And what ought then to be the Aim or End, the real disposition of the Bible student? God's word is food, bread from heaven; the first need for Bible study is:—A GREAT HUNGER AFTER RIGHTEOUSNESS,—a great desire TO DO ALL GOD'S WILL. The Bible is a light: the first condition to its enjoyment is—a HEARTY LONGING TO WALK IN GOD'S WAYS. Is not this what the texts I have placed above teach us? "Blessed are they that hear the word of God AND KEEP IT" There is no blessedness in hearing or knowing God's word apart from KEEPING IT. The word is nothing if it be not kept, obeyed, done. "If any man willeth TO DO HIS WILL, he shall KNOW." According to this saying of our Lord, all true knowledge of God's word depends upon there being first THE WILL TO DO IT. Is not this the very lesson we are enforcing. God will refuse to unlock the real meaning and blessing of His word to any but those WHOSE WILL IS DEFINITELY SET UPON DOING IT. I must read my Bible with one purpose—"Whatsoever He saith unto you, DO IT."

Why this should be so, is easily ascertained when we think of what WORDS are meant for. They stand between the will and the deed. A man wills to do something for you; before he does it, he expresses his thought or purpose in words; then he fulfils the words by doing what he has promised. Even so with God. His words have their value from what He does. In creation His word was with power: He spake and it was done. In grace He does what He says. David prays (2 Samuel vii. 25) "Do as Thou hast SPOKEN." Solomon says at the consecration of the temple—"Who hath with His hand FULFILLED that which He SPAKE with His Mouth"; "who hath PERFORMED His word that He SPAKE"; "who hast KEPT that which Thou didst PROMISE; "who SPAKE IT with Thy mouth, and hast fulfilled with Thy hand"; "let Thy word be verified, which Thou hast spoken." (2 Chron. vi. 4, 10, 15, 16.) In the prophets, God says, "I the Lord have spoken it; I WILL DO IT." And they say, "What Thou hast spoken, IS DONE." The truth and the worth of what God promises consists in this, that HE DOES IT. His word of promise is meant to be done.

This is no less true of His word of command, of things which He meant US TO DO. If we do not do them, if we seek to know them, if we admire their beauty and praise their wisdom, but do not DO THEM, we delude ourselves. They are meant TO BE DONE; it is only as we do them that their real meaning and blessing can be unfolded to us. It is only as we do them, that we really can grow in the Divine life. "Walk worthy of the Lord unto all pleasing, bearing fruit unto EVERY GOOD WORK (this first, then) and increasing IN THE KNOWLEDGE of God." It is only when we approach God's words with the same object which God had in view THAT THEY SHOULD BE DONE, that we can have any hope of blessing.

Is this not what we see all around us in the pursuit of knowledge, or in any branch of trade? The apprentice or pupil is expected to put the lessons he receives into practice; only then is he prepared for further teaching. And even so in the Christian life, Bible study is mere theory, a pleasing exercise of mind and imagination, worth little or nothing for a life of true holiness or Christlikeness, until the student be ready never to open or close his Bible without making God's purpose His very own, and hearkening when He says—"Do ALL that I SPEAK."

This was the mark of the saints of old. "So Abram went, as the Lord had spoken to him."

"As the Lord had commanded Moses, so did he," is the description of the man who as a servant was faithful in all his house. And of David we read:—"I have found a man after mine own heart, who shall do all my will." In Psalm cxix. we hear him speaking with God about His word, and praying for Divine light and teaching, but ever accompanied by the vow of obedience, or some other expression of love and delight. It is the doing of God's will, that even with God's own Son, is the one secret of entrance into the favour and the mind of God.

I have just been reading Mr. Moody's new book, "Pleasure and Profit in Bible Study." I doubt not but many will avail themselves of the suggestions it contains. They will think rightly, what has helped a man like Mr. Moody, can help me too. And yet they may be disappointed. They must be, unless they bring to the Bible what Mr. Moody brought: AN HONEST DESIRE TO DO WHATEVER HE SAW GOD WANTED HIM TO DO. Young Christian! I beseech you by the mercies of God, when you ask God to lead you into the treasures of His word, into the palace where Christ dwells, do it as one who presents himself a living sacrifice, READY TO DO WHATEVER GOD SHALL SPEAK. Do not think this a matter of course. It is of deeper importance than you know. This is more frequently absent from Bible study than you think. Seek for it with deep humility. The first need for enjoying your food is hunger. The first requirement for the Bible study is A SIMPLE, DETERMINED LONGING TO FIND OUT WHAT GOD WANTS YOU TO DO, AND A DEAD-IN-EARNEST RESOLVE TO DO IT. "If any man willeth TO DO HIS WILL, he shall know of the teaching"—to him the word of God will be opened up.

X

THE BLESSEDNESS OF THE DOER

"Be ye doers of the word, and not hearers only, deluding your own selves. But . . . being not a hearer that forgetteth, but a doer that worketh, this man shall be blessed in his doing."—JAMES i. 22-25.

WHAT a terrible delusion to be content with, to delight in hearing the word, and yet not to do it. And how terribly common, the sight of multitudes of Christians listening to the word of God most regularly and earnestly, and yet not doing it. If their own servant were to do so, hearing but NOT DOING, how summary the judgment would be. And yet, so complete is the delusion, they never know that they are not living good Christian lives. What can it be that thus deludes us?

There is more than one thing. One is that people mistake the pleasure they have in hearing, for religion and worship. The mind delights in having the truth put clearly before it; the imagination is gratified by its illustration; the feelings are stirred by its application. To an active mind knowledge gives pleasure. A man may study some branch of science—say electricity—for the enjoyment the knowledge gives him, without the least intention of applying it practically. And so people go to church, and enjoy the preaching, AND YET DO NOT DO WHAT GOD ASKS. The unconverted and the converted man alike remain content to go on in doing and confessing, and still doing the things which they ought not to do.

Another cause of this delusion is the terrible perversion of the doctrine of our impotence to good. The grace of Christ to enable us to obey, to keep from sinning and really to make us holy, is so little believed, that men practically think that there is a necessity of sinning on them. God cannot expect an exact obedience of them, for He knows they cannot render it. This error cuts away the very root of a determined purpose to do all God has said. It closes the heart to any earnest desire to believe and experience all God's grace can do in us, and keeps men self-contented in the midst of sin. Hearing and not doing—what terrible self-delusion.

There is a third reason for it, having special reference to private Bible reading. The hearing or reading is regarded as a duty, the performance of which is considered to be a religious service. We have spent our five or ten minutes in the morning reading; we have read thoughtfully and attentively; we have tried to take in what was read: a duty faithfully performed eases the conscience, and gives a sense of satisfaction. And there is hardly any conception of the worthlessness, and more than that, of the hardening influence of a duty performed or of knowledge acquired, unless we go out with our whole heart set upon LITERALLY DOING AND BEING WHAT GOD'S WORD SAYS HE WOULD HAVE US AND CAN MAKE US. Terrible delusion! "Be ye doers of the word, and not hearers only, deluding your own selves."

It is in the closet, in the morning watch, that this delusion must be fought and conquered. We may find that it will disturb our regular Bible reading, and make us fall behind in our portions. It need not do this. But far better it should, than that this point remain doubtful and unsettled. EVERYTHING DEPENDS on this. Our Lord Jesus said: "If any man willeth to DO HIS WILL, he shall KNOW OF THE TEACHING whether it be of God." It is only the heart that delights in God's law, and HAS SET ITS WILL DETERMINEDLY ON DOING IT, that can receive the divine illumination, which spiritually knows the teaching of Christ in its Divine origin and power. Without this will to do, our knowledge will not profit: it is mere head knowledge.

In life, in science and art, in business, the only way of truly knowing, is doing. What a man cannot do he does not thoroughly know. THE ONLY WAY TO KNOW GOD, TO TASTE HIS BLESSEDNESS, IS THROUGH THE DOING OF HIS WILL. That proves whether it is a God of my own sentiment and imagination that I confess, or the true and living God who rules and works all. It is only in doing His will that I prove I love it and accept it, and make myself one with it. And there is no possible way under heaven of being united to God BUT BY BEING UNITED TO HIS WILL in the doing of it. It is the quiet of the inner chamber, in the spirit in which I do my private Bible reading, in the determination with which I seek to have this point absolutely and finally settled, I AM GOING TO DO WHATEVER GOD SAYS, that the awful self-delusion of hearing and not doing must be conquered.

It may help us if we take some portion of God's Word and see how we are to deal with it.

Suppose it to be the Sermon on the Mount. I begin with the first Beatitude: "Blessed are the poor in spirit." I ask—What does this mean? Am I obeying this injunction? Am I at least thoroughly in earnest in seeking day by day to maintain this disposition? As I feel how far my proud, self-confident nature is from it, am I willing to wait, and plead with Christ, and believe that He can work it in me? Am I going TO DO THIS—to be poor in spirit? Or shall I again be a hearer and not a doer?

And so I may go through the Beatitudes, and through the whole Sermon, with its teaching on meekness and mercy, on love and righteousness, on doing everything as unto the Father, and in everything trusting Him, on doing His will and Christ's words, and verse by verse ask—Do I know what this means? Am I living it out? Am I doing it? Am I what He speaks? And as ever again, the answer comes—I fear not, nay, I see no possibility of living thus, and doing what He says, I shall be led to feel the need of an entire revision of both my creed and conduct. And I shall ask whether the vow, WHATEVER HE SAYS I AM GOING TO DO, has ever taken the place either in my Bible reading or my life which He demands that it should have.

Ere I know, such questionings may begin to work in me a poverty of spirit I never knew, and lead me to an entirely new insight into my need of a Christ who will breathe in me His own life, AND WORK IN ME ALL HE SPEAKS. I will get courage in faith to say: I CAN DO all things in Him who strengtheneth me: Whatsoever He saith in His word, I will do.

XI

KEEPING CHRIST'S COMMANDMENTS

"If ye know these things, blessed are ye if ye do them."—JOHN xiii. 17.

THE blessedness and the blessing of God's Word is only to be known BY DOING IT.

The subject is of such supreme importance in the Christian life, and therefore in our Bible study, that I must ask you to return to it once more. And let us this time just take the one expression, Keeping the Word, or keeping the commandments.

Let us take it first in the farewell discourse. You may be familiar with the passages, but it will be of use to look at them together.

"If ye love Me, KEEP MY COMMANDMENTS, and the Father will send you the Comforter" (John xiv. 15, 16).

"He that hath My commandments, AND KEEPETH THEM, he it is that loveth Me, and he shall be loved of My Father" (v. 21).

"If a man love ME, HE WILL KEEP My words, and My Father will love him" (v. 23).

"If ye abide in ME AND MY WORDS ABIDE IN YOU, ask whatsoever ye will, and it shall be done unto you" (xv. 7).

"IF YE KEEP My commandments, ye shall abide in My love" (xv. 10).

"Ye are My friends, IF YE DO WHATSOEVER I COMMAND YOU" (v. 10).

Study and compare these passages, until the words enter the heart and work the deep conviction that KEEPING CHRIST'S COMMANDMENTS IS THE INDISPENSABLE CONDITION OF ALL TRUE SPIRITUAL BLESSING. For the coming of God the Holy Spirit, and His actual indwelling, for the enjoyment of the Father's love, the inward manifestation of Christ, the abode of the Father and the Son in the heart, the power of prayer, the abiding in Christ's love, and the enjoyment of His friendship, the keeping of the commandments is the one requisite. And for the power to claim and enjoy these blessings in faith day by day, the childlike consciousness that we do keep them is indispensable too. And no less indispensable is, for fruitful Bible study, the quiet assurance that dare expect Divine light and strength with every word of God because He knows that we are ready to obey to the very utmost. THROUGH THE WILL OF GOD, DELIGHTED IN, AND DONE, LIES OUR ONLY WAY TO THE HEART OF THE FATHER, AND HIS ONLY WAY TO OUR HEART. KEEP THE COMMANDMENTS: this is the way to every blessing.

See how strikingly all this is confirmed by what we find in John's first epistle.

"Hereby do we know that we know Him, IF WE KEEP His commandments. He that saith, I know Him, and KEEPETH NOT His commandments, is a liar. But WHOSO KEEPETH His word, in him verily is the love of God perfected" (ii. 3-5). The only proof of true, living, saving knowledge of God; the only proof of not being self-deceived in our religion; of God's love not being an imagination, but a possession, is, keeping His word.

"If our heart condemn us not, we have boldness toward God; and whatsoever we ask we receive, BECAUSE WE KEEP His commandments. And HE THAT KEEPETH His commandments, abideth in Him" (iii. 21, 22, 24). Keeping the commandments is the secret of confidence toward God, and true intimate fellowship with Him.

"This is the love of God that WE KEEP His commandments, for whatsoever is begotten of God overcometh the world" (v. 3, 4). Our profession of love is worthless, except as it is proved to be true by the keeping of His commandments in the power of a life begotten of God. Knowing God, having the love of God perfected in us, having boldness with God, and abiding in Him, being begotten of Him and loving Him—all, all, is dependent on the one thing—KEEPING THE COMMANDMENTS.

It is only as we realise the prominence Christ and Scripture give to this truth, that we shall learn to give it the same prominence in our life. It will become to us one of the keys to true Bible study. The man who reads his Bible with the longing and determined purpose TO SEARCH OUT AND TO OBEY EVERY COMMANDMENT OF GOD AND OF CHRIST, is on the right track to receiving all the blessing the Word was ever meant to bring. He will specially learn two things. How he needs to wait for the teaching of the Holy Spirit to lead him into all God's will. And what blessedness there is in performing daily duties, not only because they are right, or he delights in them, but because they are the will of God. He will find how all daily life is elevated, when he says as Christ did: "This commandment received I of My Father." The Word will become the light and guide by which all his steps are ordered. And his life will become the training school in which the sanctifying power of the Word is proved, and the mind ever prepared anew for its teaching and encouragement. And so the keeping of the commandments will be the key to every spiritual blessing.

Make a determined effort to grasp what this life of full obedience means. Take some of Christ's clearest commands:—Love one another even as I have loved you; ye ought to wash one another's feet; ye should do as I have done to you: and accept a Christlike love and humility as the law of the supernatural life you are to live.

So far from the sense of failure or impotence leading you to despair, or to rest contented in what you think attainable, let it only encourage you to put your hope more entirely on Him, who by His Spirit will work in you both to will and to do.

Once again, our one aim must be perfect harmony between conscience and conduct. Every conviction must be carried out into action. Christ's commands were meant to be obeyed. If this be not done, the accumulation of Scripture knowledge only darkens and hardens, and works that satisfaction with the pleasure which the acquisition of knowledge brings, which unfits us for the Spirit's teaching.

I pray you, do not weary of my repeating so often the blessed, solemn message. In your inner chamber the question is to be decided whether you will through the day keep the commandments of Christ. And there too will be decided whether in future life you are to bear the character of a man wholly given up to know and do the will of God.

XII

LIFE AND KNOWLEDGE

"And out of the ground made the Lord God to grow the tree of life in the midst of the garden, and the tree of knowledge of good and evil."—GEN. ii. 9.

THERE are two ways of knowing things. The one is in the mind by notion or conception; I know about a thing. The other is in the life; I know by inward experience. A blind man, who is clever, may know all that science teaches about the light, by having books read to him. A child, or a savage, who has never thought what light is, yet knows it far better than the blind scholar. The latters knows all about it by thinking; the former knows it in reality by seeing and enjoying it.

It is even so in religion. The mind can form thoughts about God from the Bible, and know all the doctrines of salvation, while the inner life does not know the power of God to save. This is why we read "He that loveth not, knoweth not God; for God is love." He may know all about God and about love, he may be able to utter beautiful thoughts about it; but unless he loves, he does not know God. Only love can know God. The knowledge of God is life eternal.

God's Word is the word of life. Out of the heart are the issues of life. The life may be strong, even where knowledge in the mind is feeble. And the knowledge may be the object of most diligent pursuit and of great delight, while the life is not affected by it.

An illustration may make this plain. Suppose we could give to an apple tree understanding, with eyes to see and hands to work, this might enable the apple tree to do for itself what the gardener now does, to gather manure or bring moisture. But the inner life of the apple tree would still be the same, quite different from the understanding that had been added to it. And so the inner divine life in a man is something quite different from the intellect with which he knows about it. That intellect is indeed most needful, to offer to the heart the Word of God which the Holy Spirit can quicken. And yet it is absolutely impotent, either to impart, or quicken, the true life. It is but a servant that carries the food; it is the heart that must feed, and be nourished and live.

The two trees in Paradise are God's revelation of the same truth. If Adam had eaten of the tree of life, he would have received and known all the good God had for him in living power as an experience. And he would have known evil only by being absolutely free from it. But Eve was led astray by the desire for knowledge—"the fruit was to be desired to make one wise," and man got a knowledge of good without possessing it, a knowledge of it, only from the evil that was its opposite. And since that day man has ever sought his religion more in knowledge than in life.

It Is only Life, Experience, Possession, of God and His Goodness That Gives True Knowledge. The knowledge of the intellect cannot quicken. "Though I understand all mysteries and all knowledge, and have not love, I am nothing." It is in our daily Bible reading that this danger meets us; it is there it must be met and conquered. We need the intellect to hear and understand God's Word in its human meaning. But we need to know that the possession of the truth by the intellect cannot profit but as the Holy Spirit makes it life and truth in the heart. We need to yield our heart, and wait on God in quiet submission and faith to work in us by that Spirit. As this becomes a holy habit, we shall learn the art of intellect and heart working in perfect harmony, and each movement of the mind being ever accompanied by the corresponding movement of the heart, waiting on and listening for the teaching of the Spirit.

XIII

THE HEART AND THE UNDERSTANDING

"Trust in the Lord with all thine heart, and lean not unto thine own understanding."—PROV. iii. 5.

THE chief object of the Book of Proverbs is to teach knowledge and discretion, and to guide in the path of wisdom and understanding. To understand righteousness, to understand the fear of the Lord, to find good understanding, it is to this the Proverbs offer to guide us. But it gives the warning in the pursuit of this, to distinguish between trusting to our own understanding, and intellect, and seeking spiritual understanding, that which God gives, even an understanding heart. "Trust in the Lord with all thine heart, and lean not to thine own understanding." In all our seeking after knowledge and wisdom, in all our planning our life, or studying the Word, we have these two powers—the understanding or intellect, which knows things from without, by nature and the conceptions we form, and the heart, which knows them by experience as it takes them up into the will and affection.

I am deeply persuaded that one of the chief reasons why so much Bible teaching and Bible knowledge is comparatively fruitless, one of the chief causes of the lack of holiness, and devotion, and power in the Church, is to be found here—the trusting to our own understanding in religion. I beseech my readers to give me a patient hearing here.

Many argue: But surely God gave us our intellect, and without it there is no possibility of knowing God's Word. Most true; but listen. By the fall our whole human nature was disordered. The will became enslaved, the affections were perverted, the understanding was darkened. All admit the ruin of the fall in the two former, but practically deny it in the latter. They admit that even the believer has not in himself the power of a holy will, and needs the daily renewing of the grace of Jesus Christ. They admit that he has not the power of holy affection, loving God and his neighbour, except as it is wrought in him unceasingly by the Holy Spirit. But they do not notice that the intellect is just as much spiritually ruined and impotent, and incapable of apprehending spiritual truth. It was especially the desire for knowledge, in a way and at a time God had forbidden it, that led Eve astray, as the outcome of the temptation. To think that we can take the knowledge of God's truth for ourselves out of His word as we will, is still our greatest danger. We need a deep conviction of the impotence of our understanding really to know the truth, and of the terrible danger of self-confidence and self-deception in doing so, to see the need of the word, "Trust in the Lord with all thine heart, and lean not to thine understanding." It is with the heart man believeth. It is with all the heart we are to seek, and serve, and love God. It is only with the heart we can know God, or worship God, in spirit and truth. It is in the heart, therefore, that the Divine Word does the work. It is into our heart God hath sent forth the Spirit of His Son. It is the heart, the inward life of desire and love and will and surrender, that the Holy Spirit guides into all the truth.

In Bible study, "Trust in the Lord with all thine heart, and lean not to thine own understanding."

Trust not, wholly distrust, thy own understanding. It can only give thee thoughts and conceptions of Divine things without the reality. It will deceive thee with the thought that the truth, if received into the mind, will somehow surely enter the heart. And so it will blind thee to the terrible experience which is universal, that men daily read, and every Sunday delight to hear God's Word, and yet are made neither humble, nor holy, nor heavenly minded by it.

Instead of trusting the understanding, come with the heart to the Bible. Instead of trusting the understanding, trust in the Lord, and that with all thy heart. Let not the understanding, but the whole heart set upon the living God as the Teacher, be the chief thing, when thou enterest thy closet. Then shalt thou find good understanding. God will give thee an understanding heart, a spiritual understanding.

You may ask me, as I have been often asked, "But what am I to do? How am I to study my Bible? I see no way of doing so, but by using the understanding."

Perfectly right. But do not use it for what it cannot do. Remember two things. One is, that it can only give you a picture or thought of spiritual things. The moment it has done this, go with your heart to the Lord to make His Word life and truth in you. The other is, remember that pride of intellect, the danger of leaning to your own understanding is unceasing, and that nothing, not even the most determined purpose, can save you from this, but only the continual dependence of the heart on the Holy Spirit's teaching. It is alone through the Holy Spirit quickening the Word in the heart, in the disposition and affections, that He can guide the intellect. "The meek will He guide in judgment; the meek will He shew his way." "The fear of the Lord,"—a disposition—"is the beginning of wisdom."

With every thought from the Word the understanding grasps, bow before God in dependence and trust. Believe with the whole heart that God can and will make it true. Ask for the Holy Spirit to make it work effectually in the heart. So the Word becomes the strength of our life.

Persevere in this, and the time will come when the Holy Spirit, dwelling in the heart and life, will hold the understanding in subjection, and let His holy light shine through it.

XIV.

GOD'S THOUGHTS AND OUR THOUGHTS

"As the heavens are higher than the earth, so are my thoughts higher than your thoughts."—Is. lv. 9.

On earth the words of a wise man often mean something different from what a hearer understands of them. How natural then that the words of God, as He understands them, mean something infinitely higher than we at once apprehend.

There is very great need for remembering this. Doing so will lead us continually from resting content with our knowledge and thoughts of the Word, to wonder and wait what may be its full blessing as God has meant it. It will give our prayer for the Holy Spirit's teaching new point and urgency, even to show us what has not yet entered into our heart to conceive. It will give confidence to the hope that there is for us, even in this life, a fulfilment beyond our highest thoughts.

God's Word thus has two meanings. The one is that which it has in the mind of God, making the human words actually the bearer of all the glory of Divine wisdom, and power, and love. The other is our feeble, partial, defective apprehension of it. Even after grace and experience have made such words as the love of God, the grace of God, the power of God, or any one of the many promises connected with these verities, very true and real to us, there is still an infinite fulness in the Word we have not yet known.

How strikingly this is put in our text from Isaiah. "As the heavens are higher than the earth." Our faith in the fact is so simple and clear that no one would dream of trying with his little arm to reach the sun or the stars. To climb the highest mountain would not avail. We do with our whole heart believe it. And now God says, even so, "my thoughts are higher than your thoughts." Even when the Word has spoken out God's thoughts, and our thoughts have sought to take them in, they still remain, as high above our thoughts as the heavens are higher than the earth. All the infinities of God and the eternal world dwell in the Word as the seed of eternal life. And as the full-grown oak is so mysteriously greater than the acorn from which it sprang, so God's words are but seeds from which God's mighty wonders of grace and power can grow up.

Faith in this Word should teach us two lessons, the one of ignorance, the other of expectation. We should learn to come to the Word as little children. Jesus said, "Thou hast hid these things from the wise and prudent, and hast revealed them unto babes." The prudent and the wise are not necessarily hypocrites or enemies. There are many of God's own dear children, who, by neglecting to cultivate continually a childlike spirit, and unconsciously resting on the scripturalness of their creed, or the honesty of their Scripture study, have spiritual truth hidden from them, and never become spiritual men. "Who among men knoweth the things of a man, save the spirit of the man, which is in him? Even so the things of God none knoweth, save the Spirit of God. But we received the Spirit of God, that we might know!" Let a deep sense of our ignorance, a deep distrust of our own power of understanding the things of God even, mark our Bible study.

Then, the deeper our despair of entering aright into the thoughts of God, the greater the confidence of expectancy may be. God wants to make His Word true in us. "Thy children shall be taught of God." The Holy Spirit is already in us to reveal the things of God. In answer to our humble believing prayer God will, through Him, give an evergrowing insight into the mystery of God—our wonderful union and likeness to Christ, His living in us, and our being as He was in this world.

Yea more—if our hearts thirst and wait for it, a time may come when, by a special communication of His Spirit, all our yearnings are satisfied and Christ so takes possession of the heart, that, what was long a faith becomes an experience, that as the heavens are higher than the earth His thoughts are higher than our thoughts.

XV

MEDITATION

"Blessed is the man whose delight is in the law of the Lord, and in His law doth he meditate day and night."—Ps. i. 1, 2. (Josh. i. 8. Ps. cxix. 15, 23, 48, 78, 97, 99 and 148. 1 Tim. v. 15.) "Let the words of my mouth and the meditation of my heart be acceptable in Thy sight, O Lord."—Ps. xix. 14 and xlix. 3.

The true aim of education, study, reading, is to be found, not in what is brought into us, but in what is brought out of ourselves, by the awakening into active exercise of our inward power. This is as true of the study of the Bible, as of any other study. God's Word only works its true blessing when the truth it brings to us has stirred the inner life, and reproduced itself in resolve, trust, love, or adoration. When the heart has received the Word through the mind, and has had its spiritual powers called out and exercised on it, the Word is no longer void, but has done that whereunto God has sent it. It has become part of our life, and strengthened us for new purpose and effort.

It is in meditation that the heart holds and appropriates the Word. Just as in reflection the understanding grasps all the meaning and bearings of a truth, so in meditation the heart, assimilates it and makes it a part of its own life. We need continual reminding that the heart means the will and the affection. The meditation of the heart implies desire, acceptance, surrender, love. Out of the heart are the issues of life; what the heart truly believes, that it receives with love and joy, and allows to master and rule the life. The intellect gathers and prepares the food on which we are to feed. In meditation the heart takes it in and feeds on it.

The art of meditation needs to be cultivated. Just as a man needs to be trained to concentrate his mental powers so as to think clearly and accurately, a Christian needs to carefully consider and meditate, until the holy habit has been formed of yielding up the whole heart to every word of God.

The question sometimes is asked, how this power of meditation can be cultivated. The very first thing is to present ourselves before God. It is His Word; that Word has no power of blessing apart from Him. It is into His presence and fellowship the Word is meant to bring us. Practise His presence, and take the Word as from Himself in the assurance that He will make it work effectually in the heart. In Psalm cxix. you have the word seven times, but each time as part of a prayer addressed to God. "I will meditate in THY precepts." "Thy servant did meditate in THY statutes." "O how I love THY law, it is my meditation all the day." Meditation is the heart turning towards God with His own Word, seeking to take it up into the affection and will, into its very life.

Another element of true meditation is quiet restfulness. In our study of Scripture, in our endeavour to grasp an argument, or to master a difficulty, our intellect often needs to put forth its utmost efforts. The habit of soul required in meditation is different. Here we turn with some truth we have found, or some mystery in which we are waiting for divine teaching, to hide the word we are engaged with in the depth of the heart, and to believe that, by the Holy Spirit, its meaning and power will be revealed in our inner life. "Thou desirest truth in the inward parts; and in the hidden part thou shalt make me to know wisdom." In the description of our Lord's mother we are told: "Mary kept all these things and pondered them in her heart." In His mother keeping all these sayings in her heart, we have the image of a soul that has begun to know Christ, and is on the sure way to know Him better.

It is hardly necessary to say further that in meditation the personal application takes a prominent place. This is all too little the case with our intellectual study of the Bible. Its object is to know and understand. In meditation the chief object is to appropriate and experience. A readiness to believe every promise implicitly, to obey every command unhesitatingly, to "stand perfect and complete in all the will of God," is the only true spirit of Bible study. It is in quiet meditation that this faith is exercised, that this allegiance is rendered, that the full surrender to all God's will is made, and the assurance received of grace to perform our vows.

And then meditation must lead to prayer. It provides matter for prayer. It must lead on to prayer, to ask and receive definitely what it has seen in the Word or accepted in the Word. Its value is that it is the preparation for prayer, deliberate and whole-hearted supplication for what the heart has felt that the Word has revealed as needful or possible. That means the rest of faith, that looks upward in the assurance that the Word will open up and prove its power, in the soul that meekly and patiently gives itself away to it.

The reward of resting for a time from intellectual effort, and cultivating the habit of holy meditation, will be that in course of time the two will be brought into harmony, and all our study be animated by the spirit of a quiet waiting on God, and a yielding up of the heart and life to the Word.

Our fellowship with God is meant for all the day. The blessing of securing a habit of true meditation in the morning watch will be, that we shall be brought nearer the blessedness of the man of the first Psalm; "Blessed is the man whose delight is in the law of the Lord, and in His law doth he meditate day and night."

Let all workers and leaders of God's people

remember that they need this more than others, if they are to train them to it, and to keep up their own communication unbroken with the only source of strength and blessing. God says, "I will be with thee; I will not fail nor forsake thee. Only be thou strong and very courageous that thou mayest observe to do according to all the law . . . that thou mayest prosper whithersoever thou goest. This book of the law shall not depart out of thy mouth; THOU SHALT MEDITATE THEREIN DAY AND NIGHT . . . Then thou shalt have good success. . . . Be strong and of a good courage."

"Let the words of my mouth and the meditation of my heart, be acceptable in THY SIGHT, O Lord my Strength and my Redeemer." Let nothing less be your aim—that your meditation may be acceptable in His sight—part of the spiritual sacrifice you offer. Let nothing less be your prayer and expectation, that your meditation may be true worship, the living surrender of the heart to God's Word in His presence.

XVI

REVEALED UNTO BABES

"I thank Thee, Father, Lord of heaven and earth, that Thou hast hid these things from the wise and prudent, and revealed them unto babes."—MATT. xi. 25; LUKE x. 21.

THE wise and prudent are the men who are conscious and confident of their power of mind and reason to aid them in their pursuit of Divine Knowledge. The babes are those whose chief work is not the mind and its power, but the heart and its disposition. Ignorance, helplessness, dependence, meekness, teachableness, trust and love—these are the tempers God seeks in those whom He teaches. (Ps. xxv. 9, 12, 14, 17, 20.)

One of the most important parts of our devotions is the study of God's Word. Of what deep importance that we should ever receive the Word in the Spirit that waits for the Father to reveal its truth in us. And of what importance that we should have the child-like, yea the babe-like disposition to which the Father loves to impart the secrets of His love. With the wise and prudent head-knowledge is the first thing; from them God hides the spiritual meaning of THE VERY THING THEY THINK THEY UNDERSTAND. With the babes, not the head and its knowledge but the heart and FEELING, the sense of humility, love and trust, is the first thing, and to them God reveals, in their inner life and experience, THE VERY THING THEY KNOW THEY CANNOT UNDERSTAND.

Education tells us that there are two styles of teaching. The ordinary teacher makes the communication of knowledge his chief object, and cultivates the powers of the child as far as they help him to attain his object. The true teacher considers the amount of knowledge a secondary thing. His first aim is to develop the power of mind and spirit, and to aid the pupil, both mentally and morally, in using his powers aright in the pursuit and the application of knowledge. Even so there are two classes of preachers. Some pour forth instruction and argument and appeal unceasingly, leaving it to the hearers to make the best use they can of what is brought them. The true preacher knows how much depends upon the state of heart, and seeks, even as our Lord Jesus did, to subordinate the teaching of objective truth or doctrine to the cultivation of those dispositions without which teaching profits little. A hundred sermons, eloquent and earnest, to the wise and prudent, to Christians who listen with the thought that they can understand, and that what they hear will somehow profit them, will bring less real blessing, than one sermon to hearers in whom the preacher has awakened a consciousness of spiritual ignorance, a babe-like docile spirit that waits for and depends on, that truly accepts and obeys, the Father's teaching.

In the secret chamber every man is, as far as human aid is concerned, his own teacher and preacher. He is to train himself in the blessed habit of babe-like simplicity and teachableness. Remembering that it was not only needful that Divine Truth should be revealed in the world, but that there must be an individual revelation to each, by the Holy Spirit, his first care is to wait on the Father to reveal to him, and within him, the hidden mystery in its power in the inner life. In this posture he exercises the babe-like spirit, and receives the Kingdom as a little child. All Evangelical Christians believe in regeneration. How few believe that when a man is born of God, A BABE-LIKE DEPENDENCE ON GOD FOR ALL TEACHING AND STRENGTH OUGHT TO BE HIS CHIEF CHARACTERISTIC. It was the one thing our Lord Jesus insisted on above all. When He pronounced the poor in heart, the meek, the hungry, "blessed," when He called men to learn of Him that He was meek and lowly in heart, when He spoke so often of our humbling ourselves and becoming as little children, it was because the first and chief mark of being a child of God, of being like Jesus Christ, is AN ABSOLUTE DEPENDENCE UPON GOD FOR EVERY BLESSING, AND SPECIALLY FOR ANY REAL KNOWLEDGE OF SPIRITUAL THINGS. Let each ask himself: Have I counted the babe-like spirit the first essential in my Bible study? Of what use is Bible study without the babe-like spirit? It is the real and only key to God's school. Would it not be well to set aside everything to secure this? Then alone will God reveal His hidden wisdom.

The new birth, being begotten of God, by which we become God's children, is meant to make us babes. It will give us the child-spirit as well as the child-teaching. It cannot do the second without the first. Let us believe and yield ourselves to the new life in us, to the leading of the Spirit; He will breathe in us the spirit of little children. The first object of Bible study is to learn the hidden wisdom of God. The first condition of obtaining this knowledge, is to accept the fact that God Himself reveals it to us.

The first disposition needed for receiving that revelation is a babe-like spirit. We all know how the first thing a wise workman does is to see that he has the proper tools, and that they are in proper order. He does not count it lost time to stop his work and sharpen the tools. It is not lost time to let the Bible study wait, till you see whether you are in the right position—waiting for the Father's revelation in the meek and babe-like spirit. If you feel that you have not read your Bible in this spirit, confess and forsake at once the self-confident spirit of the wise and prudent. Not only pray for the babe-like spirit, but believe for it. It is in you, though neglected and suppressed; you may begin at once as a child of God to experience it.

Seek not by reflection or argument to bring this babe-like spirit into your heart. Work from within outwards. It is in you, as a seed, in the new life, born of the Spirit. It must rise and grow in you as a birth of the indwelling Spirit. In this faith you must not only pray, but pray also very specially for this grace of the Spirit, and exercise it. Live as a babe before God. As a new-born babe desire the milk of the Word.

And beware of trying to assume this state of mind only when you want to study Scripture. It must be the permanent habit of your mind, the state of your heart. Then alone can you enjoy the continual guidance of the Holy Spirit.

XVII

LEARNING OF CHRIST

"Take My yoke upon you and learn of Me: for I am meek and lowly of heart; and ye shall find rest to your souls."—MATT. xi. 29.

ALL Bible study is learning. All Bible study to be fruitful should be learning of Christ. The Bible is the school book, Christ is the Teacher. It is He who opens the understanding, and opens the heart, and opens the seals. (Luke xxiv. 45, Acts xvi. 14, Rev. v. 9.) Christ is the living eternal Word, of which the written words are the human expression. Christ's presence and teaching are the secret of all true Bible study. The written Word is powerless, except as it helps us to the Living Word. No one has ever thought of accusing our Lord of not honouring the Old Testament. In His own life He proved that He loved it as coming out of the mouth of God. He ever pointed the Jews to it as the revelation of God and the witness to Himself. But with the disciples it is remarkable how frequently He spoke of His own teaching as what they most needed, and had to obey. It was only after His resurrection, when the union with Himself had been effected, and they had already received the first breathings of the Spirit (Jno. xx. 22) that we find Him expounding the Scriptures. The Jews had their self-made interpretation of the Word: they made it the greatest barrier between themselves and Him of whom it spake. It is often so with Christians too; our human apprehension of Scripture, fortified as it may be by the authority of the Church, or our own circle, becomes the greatest hindrance in the way of Christ's teachings. Christ the Living Word, seeks first to find His place in our heart and life, to be our only Teacher: thus shall we learn of Him to honour and understand Scripture.

LEARN OF ME FOR I AM MEEK AND LOWLY OF HEART. Our Lord here opens up the inmost secret of His own inner life. That which He brought down to us from heaven: that which fits Him to be a Teacher and a Saviour; that which He has given to us, and which He wants us to learn of Him: you find it all in the words, "I am meek and lowly of heart." It is the one virtue that makes Him the Lamb of God, our suffering Redeemer, our heavenly Teacher and Leader. It is the one disposition which He asks of us in coming to learn from Him: out of this all else will come. For our Bible study and all our Christian life you have here the one condition of truly learning of Christ. He, the Teacher, meek and lowly of heart, wants to make you what He is, because that is salvation. As a learner you must come and study and believe in Him the meek and lowly One, and seek to learn of Him how to he meek and lowly too.

And why is this the first and all-important thing? Because it lies at the root of the true relationship of the creature to God. God alone has life and goodness and happiness. As the God of Love He delights to give and work everything in us. Christ became the Son of Man to show in what blessed unceasing dependence upon God man is to live: this is the meaning of His being lowly in heart. It is in this spirit that angels veil their faces and cast their crowns before God. God is everything to them, and they delight to receive all and to give all. This is the root of the true Christian life: to be nothing before God and men; to wait on God alone; to delight in, to imitate, to learn of Christ, the Meek and Lowly One. This is the very key to the School of Christ, the only key to the true knowledge of Scripture. It is in this character that Christ has come to teach: it is in this character alone you can learn of Him. How little in the Christian Church, humility, the meek and lowly heart, has had the place that it has in the life of Christ and the teachings of God's Word. I am deeply persuaded that this lack lies at the root of a very large part of the feebleness and unfruitfulness of which we hear. It is only as we are meek and lowly in heart, that Christ can teach us by His Spirit what God has for us, and that God will work in us. Let each of us begin with ourselves and count this as the first condition of discipleship, and the first lesson the Master will most surely teach us. Let us make all our Bible study a learning of Christ, a trusting Him, who is so meek and gentle and kind, a waiting for Him, to work His own spirit and likeness in us. In due time our morning watch will be the scene of daily fellowship and daily blessing.

I know what difficulties I have to contend with in pleading thus that the meek and lowly heart be made the first consideration in Bible study. It is hard to make men realise that, in intercourse with God, disposition and character are everything. It is harder to show them that of all Christian disposition and character, a meek and lowly heart is the very seed and root. It is hard to convince them that without it the profit of Bible study is very little. It is above all hard to lead them to understand and believe that the meek and lowly heart is to be had, because it is the very thing Christ offers to give, teaching us how to find and receive it in Himself. In face even of all these difficulties, I, nevertheless, urge all Bible students, thoughtfully and prayerfully to enquire whether the very first question to be settled in the inner chamber is not this: Is my heart in the state in which my Teacher desires it to be? And if it be not, is not my first work to yield myself to Him to work it in me?

XVIII

TEACHABLENESS

"Take My yoke upon you and learn of Me: for I am meek and lowly of heart; and ye shall find rest to your souls."—Matt. xi. 29.

THE first virtue of a pupil is docility and willingness to be taught. What does this imply? A consciousness of his own ignorance, a readiness to give up his own way of thinking or of doing, and to look at things from the teacher's standpoint, a quiet confidence that the master knows and will show him how to learn to know too. The meek and lowly spirit listens carefully to know what the teacher's will is, and at once hastens to carry it out. If this be the spirit in a pupil it must be the teacher's fault if he does not learn.

And how is it that, with Christ as our teacher, there is with many, so much failure, so little real growth in spiritual knowledge? So much hearing and reading of the Bible, so much profession of faith in it as our only rule of life, and yet such a lack of the manifestation of its spirit and its power? So much often of honest, earnest application in the closet and the Bible circle, with but little of the joy and strength God's Word could give?

The question is one of the utmost importance. There must be some cause why there are so many disciples of Jesus who think they honestly desire to know and do His will, and who yet by their own confession and the evidence of those around them, are not holding forth the word of life as a light in the world. If the answer could be found to the question, their lives might be changed.

Our text suggests the answer: "Take My yoke upon you and learn of Me; for I am meek and lowly of heart; and ye shall find rest to your souls." Many have taken Christ as a Saviour BUT NOT AS A TEACHER. They have put their trust in Him as the Good Shepherd who gave His life for the sheep; they know little of the reality of His daily shepherding His flock, calling every one by name, or of thus hearing His voice and following Him alone. They know little of what it is to follow the Lamb; before everything to receive from Him the lamb nature, and to seek like Him to be meek and lowly in heart. It was by their three years' course in His school that Christ's disciples were fitted for the baptism of the Holy Spirit, and the fulfilment of all the wonderful promises He had given them. IT IS UNDER THE PERSONAL TEACHING OF OUR LORD JESUS, AND THROUGH THAT DOCILITY OF THE MEEK AND LOWLY HEART, WHICH DAILY WAITS FOR AND RECEIVES AND FOLLOWS THAT TEACHING, that we can truly find rest to our souls. All the weariness and burden of strain and failure and disappointment, then gives way to that divine peace which knows that all is being cared for by Christ Himself.

That taking of Christ's yoke and learning of Him His meekness and lowliness of heart, and with that, the teachableness that refuses to know or do aught in its own wisdom, is to be the spirit of our whole life, every day and all the day. But it is especially in the morning hour that this is to be cultivated, and deliverance sought from self and all its energy. It is there, while occupied with the words of God and of Christ and of the Holy Spirit, that we need daily to realise that these only profit as they lead to, and are opened up by, the personal teaching of Christ. It is there that we daily need to experience that only as the living Lord Jesus "in whom all the fulness dwells," in whom all our life and salvation are gathered up, HIMSELF COMES NEAR AND TAKES CHARGE OF US, that His teaching can be received. And it is there that we must definitely ask and cultivate the teachableness that takes up His yoke and learns of Him. Once again, the teachableness is everything. If it be true of the Holy Spirit who dwells in us, the Spirit of Christ Jesus, "He shall teach you all things," and if His whole life and work in us is a Divine teaching, it is equally true that our whole life must be a Divine teachableness. So only, can our daily intercourse with God's Word, and our daily life be what our Lord Jesus can make it.

Unlearning is often the most important part of learning: wrong impressions, prejudices and prepossessions are insuperable obstacles in the way of learning. Until these have been removed the teacher labours in vain. The knowledge he communicates only touches the surface: deep under the surface the pupil is guided by that which has become a second nature to him. The first work of the teacher is to discover, to make the pupil see and remove, these hindrances.

There can be no true and faithful learning of Christ where we are not ready to unlearn. By heredity, by education, by tradition, we have our thoughts about religion and God's Word, which are often the greater hindrance in proportion to our assurance that they are indeed the truth. To learn of Christ needs a willingness to subject every truth we hold to His inspection for criticism and correction.

Humility is the root virtue of the Christian life. The law is absolute in God's Kingdom—"He that humbleth himself shall be exalted." Our disappointment in striving after higher degrees of grace, faith, spiritual knowledge, love to souls and power to bless, is all owing to this. We have not accepted the humility of Christ as the beginning and the perfection of His salvation. "God giveth grace to the humble" has a far wider and deeper application than we think.

Docility is one form of humility. In the morning watch we place ourselves as learners in Christ's school; let docility, let humility be the distinguishing mark of the learner, and, if we feel how little we have of it, let us listen to the voice that says, "Take My yoke upon you," and, for all that this implies—"learn of Me, for I am meek and lowly of heart. And ye shall find rest to your souls."

XIX

THE LIFE AND THE LIGHT

"In the beginning was the Word. And the Word was God. In Him was life. And the Life was the Light of men."—JOHN i. 1, 4.

"He that followeth Me shall not walk in darkness, but shall have the Light of Life."—JOHN viii. 12.

BECAUSE Christ was God, He could be the Word of God. Because He had the Life of God in Himself, He could be the revealer of that Life. And so as the Living Word He is the Life-giving Word. The written word can be made void and of none effect where human wisdom is trusted for its apprehension. It is only as it is accepted as the seed in which the life of the Living Word lies hid, to be quickened by the Holy Spirit, that it can be to us the word of life. Our intercourse with God's written word ought ever to be inspired and regulated by the faith of the Eternal Word, who was God.

The same truth comes out in the expression that follows: The life is the light. When we see the light shining, we know that there is fire burning in some form or other. And so in the spiritual world. There must be life ere there can be light. There may be reflected light from a dead or dark object. There may be a borrowed light without life. But true life can alone show true light. He that follows Christ shall have the light of life.

These two statements of one great truth strikingly confirm what we learnt about the Spirit of God. Even as He knows the things of God because He is the life of God, so Christ is the Word because He is God, and has the life of God; and so the light of God only shines where the life of God is. All three thoughts bring us again to our Bible study with the one blessed, but so needful lesson, that it is only as the written word brings us the life of the Eternal Word, as its light within the heart is the shining of a life that is working there, as the Holy Spirit who knows the things of God because He is the life of God, makes them life and truth within us, can our study of Scripture really bless us.

And so we come back to the one great lesson the Spirit seeks to enforce in regard to God's Word—that IT IS ONLY AS SCRIPTURE IS RECEIVED OUT OF THE LIFE OF GOD INTO OUR LIFE THAT THERE IS ANY REAL KNOWLEDGE OF IT. It is a seed that bears within it the Divine life: where it is received in the good soil of a heart that hungers for that life, it will spring up and bring forth fruit, like all seed, "after its kind." It will reproduce in our life the very life of God, out of which it came, the very likeness and disposition of the Father and the Son through the Holy Spirit. We want to turn all this to practical account and to apply it directly to our private Bible reading.

You want to know how to begin. The rules are very simple.

The first: "Be still and know that I am God." Take time to be quiet and to realise God. "Hold thy peace at the presence of the Lord." "Be silent before the Lord." "The Lord is in His Holy temple; let all the earth keep silence before Him." Worship and wait on Him that He may speak to thee. The next: Remember that the word comes out of the life, the heart of God carrying His life to impart it to thine. Nothing less than the life of God is it: nothing less than the power of God can make it live in thee. The next: believe in Christ the Living Word. "In Him was life, and the life—His life, was the light of men." "He that followeth ME shall have the light of life." Follow Jesus in love and longing desire, in obedience and service, and so His life will work in thee, and the life shall be the light of thy soul.

And then, ask the Father for the Holy Spirit WHO ALONE KNOWETH the things of God, to make the word in thy heart living and active. Hunger for the will of God as thy daily food; thirst for the living spring of the Spirit within thee; receive the word into thy will, thy life, thy joy—the life it brings will give the light with which it shines.

The reason I have so often insisted upon the truth put forward in the last few chapters is very simple. My own experience has taught me how long it is before we clearly apprehend that the word of God must be received into the life and not only into the mind, and how long again even after we apprehend it, before we fully believe and act it out. "To write the same thing to you is not grievous to me, and for you it is profitable." Study the lesson till you know it. The word comes out of the life of God, carries that life in itself, seeks to enter my life and fill it with the life of God. This life is the light of men, and gives the light of the knowledge of the glory of God.

You may find that this lesson takes more time than you think, that it hinders you more than it helps in your Bible lessons, and that it grows all the more difficult the longer you study it. Be not afraid or impatient; but be assured that if you learn it aright, you will bless God that it has become a key you never had before, to the hidden treasure of the word, giving you true wisdom in the hidden part.

So I repeat again the simple words so inexhaustibly blessed and true. As the Spirit that lives in God alone knows the things of God, IT IS ALONE THE SPIRIT LIVING IN ME, THAT CAN MAKE ME KNOW THE THINGS OF GOD BY IMPARTING THEM TO MY LIFE

As Christ was the Word because He was God, and had the life of God, the written word can only bless me as, through it, the living Word brings the life of God unto me. As the life was in Christ, and as the Life is the Light of men, so it is only as I have the life of Christ through the word that I have the light of the knowledge of God.

XX

THE BIBLE STUDENT

"Blessed is the man whose delight is in the law of the Lord; and in His law doth he meditate day and night."—Ps. i. 1, 2.

THERE is a loud call on every side for more, for truer, Bible study. Evangelists like Mr. Moody and many others, have proved what power there is in preaching drawn directly from God's word, and inspired by the faith of its power. Earnest Christians have asked: "Why cannot our ministers speak in the same way, giving the very word of God a larger place?" Many a young minister has come away from the Theological Hall, confessing that he had been taught everything but the knowledge of how to study the Word himself, and then to stir up and help others to study it. In some of our Churches, the desire has been expressed to supply this need in the training of ministers. It might appear a very simple thing to find good men to undertake the work; and yet it has been found difficult for men with theological training to turn to the simplicity and directness of appeal to God's Word, which is needed to show younger men the way to make Scripture the one source of their knowledge and teaching. In the Students' Movement of our day, God be praised,

Bible study has had the place of prominence given to it. There is a wonderful opportunity, as there is a very great need, for so guiding it that it may bring a full blessing to the individual lives, by giving God's word its true place in the work to be done for Him. Let us look at the principles underlying the demand for more Bible study, and in faithfulness to which alone, it can be truly carried out.

1. God's Word Is the Only Authentic Revelation of God's Will. All human statements of Divine truth, however correct, are defective and carry a measure of human authority. In the Word, the voice of God speaks to us directly. Every child of God is called to direct intercourse with the Father, through the Word. As God reveals all His heart and grace in it, His child can, if he receives it from God, get all the life and power there is in the Word into his own heart and being. We know how few second-hand reports of messages or events can be fully trusted. Very few men report accurately what they have heard. Every believer has the right and calling, to stand in direct communication with God. It is in the Word God has revealed, it is in the Word He still reveals, Himself to each individual.

2. This Word of God Is a Living Word. It Carries a Divine Quickening Power in It. The human expression of the truth is often a mere conception or image of the truth, appealing to the mind and having little or no effect. The

faith of its being God's own word and of the presence and power in it, makes it effectual. All life or spirit creates for itself a form in which it is made manifest. The words in which God has chosen to clothe His own Divine thoughts are God-breathed and the life of God dwells in them. God is not the God of the dead but of the living. The word was not only inspired when first given: the Spirit of God still breathes in it. God is still in and with His word. Christians and teachers need to believe this. It will lead them to give the simple Divine word a confidence that no human teaching may have.

3. God Himself alone Can, and Most Surely Will, Be the Interpreter of His Own Word. Divine truth needs a Divine Teacher. Spiritual apprehension of spiritual things can only come of the Holy Spirit. The deeper the conviction of the unique character of the word, essentially different from, and infinitely exalted above, all merely human apprehension, the more urgently will the need be felt of a supernatural, a directly Divine, teaching. And all the more will the blessing be wrought which is the great purpose of the word. The soul will be brought to seek God Himself, and it will be led to find Him in the Holy Spirit who dwells in the heart. As that Spirit, in whom God, so wonderfully, has entered our very life and identified Himself with it, is waited on and trusted, He will make us to know wisdom in the hidden part, in the heart and disposition. The

word prayerfully read and cherished in the heart in this faith, will through the Spirit, be both light and life within us.

4. The Word Then Brings Us into the Closest and Most Intimate Fellowship with God—Unity of Will and Life. In the word God has revealed His whole heart and all His will: in His law and precepts what He wills us to do: in His redemption and His promises what He wills to do for us. As we accept that will in the word as from God Himself, and yield ourselves to its working, we learn to know God in His will, in the power of which He works in us, and in which His condescending love is known. And the word works out His richest purpose as it fills us with the reverence and dependence that comes from the Divine presence and nearness. Nothing less than this must be our aim, may be our experience, in all our Bible study.

Let us now take these four thoughts over again and make the practical application.

In Holy Scripture we have the very words in which the Holy God has spoken and in which He speaks to us.

These words are, to-day, full of the life of God. God is in them, and makes His presence and power known to them who seek Him in them.

To those who ask and wait for the teaching of the Holy Spirit who dwells within us, the Spirit will reveal the spiritual meaning and power of the word.

The word is thus meant every day to be the means of the revelation of God Himself to the soul and of fellowship with Him.

Have we learnt to apply these truths? Do we understand that the word ever says "Seek God. Hearken to God. Wait for God. God will speak to you. Let God teach you?" All we hear about more Bible teaching and Bible study must lead to this one thing. We must be men, and we must help to train others to be men, with whom THE WORD IS NEVER SEPARATED FROM THE LIVING GOD HIMSELF, AND WHO LIVE AS MEN TO WHOM GOD IN HEAVEN SPEAKS EVERY DAY AND ALL DAY.

XXI

WHO ART THOU?

" Set your mind on the things that are above, . . . for ye died and your life is hid with Christ in God."—COL. iii. 2, 3. R. V.

IN entering into God's presence in the morning hour much depends upon the Christian realising not only who God is, but WHO HE HIMSELF IS, and what the relation in which he stands to God. To the question " Who art thou? " which is asked, not in words but in spirit, of each one who claims right of access and an audience from the Most High, there must be an answer ready in his inmost consciousness; that consciousness must be nothing less than a living sense of the place he has in Christ before God. The mode of expressing it may differ at different times, in substance it will always be the same.

Who am I? yes, let me think and say, who I am who now come to ask that God shall meet me here, shall spend this whole day with me? I am one who knows, by the word and Spirit of God, that I am in Christ, and that my life is hid with Christ in God. In Christ I died to sin and the world. I am now taken out of them, separated from them, and delivered from their power. I have been raised together with Christ and in Him

I live unto God. My life is hid with Christ in God and I come to God to claim and obtain all Divine life that is hidden away in Him for to-day's need and supply.

Yes, this is who I am, I say it to God in humble, holy reverence, as my plea. I say it to myself to encourage others, as well as myself, to seek and expect nothing less—grace to live out, here on earth, the hidden life of heaven. I am one who longs to say, who does say, Christ is my life. The longing of my soul is for Christ, revealed by the Father Himself within the heart. Nothing less can satisfy me. My life is hid with Christ. He can be my life no other way than as He is in my heart. Yes! with nothing less can I be content than Christ in the heart. Christ is a Saviour from sin. Christ as the gift and bringer of God's love. Christ as an indwelling Friend and Lord.

Oh! my God! if Thou dost ask, "Who art thou?" listen to my stammering: I live in Christ and Christ in me. Thou alone canst make me know and be all it means.

There is more I shall have to say, as my plea for the grace of God's presence and power all the day. I come as one who desires, who seeks, to be prepared to live out the life of Christ to-day on earth, to translate His hidden heavenly glory, into the language of daily life, with its dispositions and its duties. As the Christ on earth lived only to do the will of God, it is my great desire to stand perfect and complete in all His will. My ignorance of that will, in all its spiritual application to intercourse with the world and men, is very great. My impotence is still greater. And yet I come to God as one who dare not offer less or seek any compromise, as one who in all honesty accepts the high calling of living out fully the will of God in all things.

It is this brings me to the closet. As I think of all my failures in fulfilling God's will, as I look forward to all the temptations and dangers that await me, as I feel my entire insufficiency and yet say to God—I come to claim the life hid in Christ, that I may live the life for Christ; I feel urged and drawn not to be content without the quiet assurance that God will go with me and bless me.

Who am I that I should ask these great and wonderful things of God?

May I indeed expect to live the life hid with Christ in God, so as to make it manifest in my mortal body? I may; for it is God Himself will work it in me by the Holy Spirit dwelling in me. The same God who raised Christ from the dead, and then set Him at His right hand, has raised me with Him and given me the Spirit of the glory of His Son in my heart. A life in Christ, given up to know and do all God's will, is the life God Himself will work and maintain increasingly in me by the Holy Spirit. And when I come in the morning and present myself before Him to take up afresh the life He has hidden in Himself for me, where His Son is hidden, and live it out in the flesh, I can wait confidently and quietly, as one in whom the Spirit dwells, for the Father to give the fresh anointing that teacheth all things, and Himself to take charge of the new day He has given me.

My brother, I am sure you feel of what infinite importance it is, if the morning hour is to secure God's presence for the day, that you take firm stand on nothing less than the ground of a full redemption. Believe what God says to you. Accept what God has bestowed on you in Christ. Be consciously and openly what God has made you to be. Take time before God to know it and say it. How much in a battle depends upon an impregnable position. Take your place WHERE GOD HAS PLACED YOU.

The very attempt to do this, may at times interfere with your ordinary Bible study, or prayer. It will be no loss. It will be fully recompensed later. Your life depends upon knowing who your God is, AND WHO YOU ARE AS HIS REDEEMED ONE IN CHRIST. The life of every day depends on it; when once you have learned the secret, it will, even when you do not think of it, be the strength of your heart, both in going in to God, and going out with Him to the world.

XXII

THE WILL OF GOD

"Thy will be done on earth as it is in heaven."—MATT. vi. 10.

1. The will of God is the living power to which the world owes its existence. Through that will, and according to that will, it is what it is. It is the expression or manifestation or embodiment of that Divine Will in its wisdom, power and goodness. It has, in beauty and glory, but what it owes to God's having willed it. As that Will formed it, so it upholds it every day. Creation thus does what it was destined for, it shows forth the glory of God. "They gave glory to Him that liveth for ever and ever, saying, Thou art worthy to receive glory, for Thou hast created all things, and because of Thy will they are, and were created."

2. This is true of inanimate nature. It is still more true of intelligent creatures. The Divine Will undertook the creation of a creature will in its own image and likeness, with the living power to know and accept and co-operate with that Will to which it owed its being. The blessedness of the unfallen angels, consists in counting it their highest honour and happiness to be able to will and

do exactly what God wills and does. The glory of heaven is that God's will is done there. The sin and misery of fallen angels and men, consists simply in their having turned away from, and refused to abide in, and to do, the will of God.

3. Redemption is nothing but the restoration of God's will to its place in the world. To this end Christ came and SHOWED IN A HUMAN LIFE, HOW MAN HAS BUT ONE THING TO LIVE FOR, THE DOING OF GOD'S WILL. He showed us how there was one way of conquering self-will—by a death to it, in obeying God's will even unto death. So He atoned for our self-will and conquered it for us, and opened a path through death and resurrection, into a life entirely united with, and devoted to, the will of God.

4. God's redeeming will is now able to do in fallen man, what His creating will had wrought and ever works in nature, or in unfallen beings. In Christ and His example, GOD HAS REVEALED THE DEVOTION TO AND THE DELIGHT IN HIS WILL, WHICH HE ASKS AND EXPECTS OF US. In Christ and His Spirit He renews and takes possession of our will: works in it both to will and to do, making us able and willing to do all His will.

He Himself worketh all things after the counsel of His will. "He makes us perfect in every good thing to do His will, working in us that which is pleasing in His sight." As this is revealed by the Holy Spirit, and believed, and received into the heart, we begin to get an insight into the prayer, "Thy will be done on earth as it is in heaven," and the true desire is awakened for the life it promises.

5. How essential it is to the believer that he realise his relations to God's will, and its claim on him.

Many, many, believers have no conception of what their faith or their feeling ought to be in regard to the will of God. How few who say: MY WHOLE THOUGHT OF BLESSEDNESS IS IN NOTHING BUT THE MOST COMPLETE HARMONY WITH THE WILL OF GOD. I feel my one need to be, the ever maintained surrender, not, in the very least thing, ever to do other than what God wills me to do. By God's grace every hour of my life may be a living in the will of God, and doing it as it is done in heaven.

6. It is only as a living faith in the Divine Will, working out its purposes increasingly in us, masters the heart, that we shall have the courage to believe in the answer to the prayer our Lord taught us. It is only as we see, that it is through Jesus Christ, that this working of God's will in us is carried out, that we shall understand how it is the close union to Him that gives the confidence that God will work all in us. And it is only this confidence in God, through Jesus Christ, that will assure us, that we too can do our part, and that our feeble will on earth can truly ever correspond and co-operate with the will of God. Let us but accept our destiny and our obligation as the one

thing our heart desires, that in everything the will of God be done in us and by us, as it is done in heaven; that faith will overcome the world.

7. The will may not be disconnected from its living union with the Father here, nor the living presence of the Blessed Son. It is only by a divine guidance given through the Holy Spirit, that the will of God in its beauty, in its application to daily life, in its ever-growing revelation, can be truly known. This teaching will be given, not to the wise and prudent, but to the babes, the men of child-like disposition, who are willing to wait for and depend on what is given them. The Divine guidance will lead in the path of God's will.

8. Our secret intercourse with God is the place where we repeat and learn the great lessons. . . .

The God whom I worship asks of me perfect union with His will. . . . My worship means: "I delight to do Thy Will, O God." . . . The morning hour, the inner chamber, the secret intercourse with God, as in these the knowledge of God's will, the power to perform it, the entire and joyful surrender to do all God wills, are sought and cultivated, our study of God's word and our prayer will bring their true and full blessing.

XXIII

FEEDING ON THE WORD

"Thy words were found and I did eat them; and Thy word was unto me the joy and rejoicing of my heart."—Jer. xv. 16.

Here you have three things. The Finding of God's word. This only comes to those who seek diligently for it. Then the Eating. This means the personal appropriation for our own sustenance, the taking up into our being the words of God. "Man shall not live by bread alone, but by every word that proceedeth out of the mouth of God." And then the Rejoicing, "The Kingdom of Heaven is like unto treasure hid in a field which, when a man hath found, he hideth, and for joy thereof goeth and selleth all that he hath, and buyeth that field." There we have the finding, and the appropriating, and the rejoicing. "Thy words Were Found, and I Did Eat them, and Thy word was the Joy and Rejoicing of my heart."

Eating is here the central thought. It is preceded by the searching and finding: it is accompanied and followed by the rejoicing. It is the only aim and use of the one; it is the only cause and life of the other. In the secrecy of the inner chamber how much depends on this—I DID EAT them!

To realise the difference between this and the finding of God's words, compare the corn a man may have stored in his granary, with the bread he has on his table. All the diligent labour he has bestowed in sowing and harvesting and garnering his grain, all the rich reward he has had for his care, cannot profit him, except as he feeds on the daily portion of the bread his body requires. In the finding, the harvesting, and garnering, the greater the quantity and the speedier the work—these were the things to be looked at. In the eating, the very opposite takes place—here it is the small quantity, and the slow and unceasing continuance, that characterises the appropriation. Do you see the application of this to your Scripture study in the morning watch? You need TO FIND God's words, and by careful thought to master them, so as to have them stored in mind and memory for your own use, and that of others. In this work there may often be great joy, the joy of harvest or of victory; the joy of treasure secured, or difficulties overcome; and yet we must remember this finding and possessing the words of God is not yet that eating of them which alone brings Divine life and strength to the soul.

The fact of being occupied with, and possessing good wholesome corn, will not nourish a man. The fact of being deeply interested in the knowledge of God's word will not of itself nourish the soul. "Thy words were found" that was the first thing. "And I did eat them"—that brought the joy and rejoicing.

And what is this eating? The corn which the husbandman had grown and rejoiced in as his very own, could not nourish his life, until he took it up and ate it, and so completely assimilated it, that it became part of himself, entering into his blood, forming his very bone and flesh. This has to be done in a small quantity at a time, two or three times a day, every day of the year. This is the law of eating. It is not the amount of truth I gather from God's word; it is not the interest or success of my Bible study; it is not the increased clearness of view or largeness of grasp I am obtaining, that secure the health and growth of the spiritual life. By no means. All this often leaves the nature very much unsanctified and unspiritual with very little of the holiness or humility of Christ Jesus: something else is needed. Jesus said: MY MEAT IS TO DO the will of Him that sent me. Taking a small portion of God's word, some definite command or duty of the new life, quietly receiving it into the will and the love of the heart, yielding the whole being to its rule, and vowing, in the power of the Lord Jesus, to perform it: this, and then GOING TO DO IT, this is eating the word, taking it so into our inmost being, that it becomes a constituent part of our very life. The same with a truth, or a promise; what you have eaten now becomes part of yourself, you carry it with you where you go as part of the life you live.

You see at once how the two points of difference between the corn in the granary and the bread on the table, cover all your Bible study. The gathering of Scripture knowledge is one thing. The eating of God's word, the receiving it into your very heart by the power of the life-giving Spirit, is something very different. And you see how the two laws of eating the food, in contrast to those of finding it, must always be obeyed. You can gather and garner grain to last for years. You cannot swallow a large enough quantity of bread to last for days. Day by day, and more than once a day, you take your day's food. And so the eating of God's word must be in small portions, just as much as the soul can each time receive and digest. And this, day by day, from one end of the year to the other.

It is such feeding on the word which will enable me to say: "And Thy word was the joy and rejoicing of my heart." George Muller says that he learned that he ought not to stop reading the Word until he felt happy in God: then he felt fit to go out to his day's work.

XXIV

HOLIDAYS

"If the master of the house had known in what hour the thief was coming he would have watched and not left his house to be broken through."—LUKE xii. 39.

IN an address on Education Edward Thring says: "The mighty leisure hours with their occupations are all-powerful. . . . The mighty question of leisure hours ought to be the most important question of all since it affects the character most. . . . Leisure hours are the hinge on which true education turns." This great master in the science of education had seen, that noble character, and truth of being, come first, and then after that, as second, the training of skill and strength. He had seen, too, that while a teacher can do much in word and deed by high belief and true work to stimulate and to guide, every boy has to work out his own character. And because it is in the leisure hours, when free from constraint and observation, that the boy shows what is really uppermost within him, that he spoke of the leisure hours as all-important and all-powerful, the hinge on which true education turns.

In religion this is intensely true. Thousands of

students have felt it, without knowing how to express or explain it. At college or school their morning watch has had its place in their time table. The whole mind is braced up to regular and systematic work, and the time for devotion is as duly kept as that for a class or private study.

When the time of relaxation comes, and one is free to do exactly as one likes, many a one finds that the morning watch and its fellowship with God had not become so natural, such a necessity of the spiritual life and such joy, that its observance could not interfere with our holiday pleasure. The holiday becomes the test of character, the proof of how far one could say with Job, "I have esteemed the words of thy mouth more than my necessary food." The question of leisure hours is indeed all important. In them I turn freely and naturally to what I love most. In them I prove and increase the power to hold what I have.

A teacher in a large school in America is reported to have said, "the greatest difficulty with which we have to contend is the summer vacation. Just when we have brought a boy up to a good point of discipline, and he responds to the best ideals, we lose him, and when he comes back in the autumn, we have to begin and do it all over. The summer holiday simply demoralises him." This statement, referring to ordinary study and duty, is strong: within certain limits it is no less applicable to the religious life. The sudden relaxation of regular habits, and the subtle thought that perfect liberty to do as one likes means perfect happiness, throws many a young student back in his Christian life. There is no point at which it is more needful that older and more experienced members of the Students' Association should help and guard their younger members than this. The attainment of months may be lost by the neglect of a week. We know not in what hour the thief cometh. The spirit of the morning watch means unceasing vigilance all the day and every day.

There are various aspects in which the danger, and safety from it, may be put before the student. With the holiday we are set free from the school laws under which we live during our stay there. But there are other laws: laws of morality, laws of health, from which there is no relaxation. Let the student be warned that the call to daily fellowship with God belongs not to the former but the latter class. As much as he needs every day during the holidays to eat and breathe, he needs EVERY DAY TO EAT THE BREAD AND BREATHE THE AIR OF HEAVEN.

Make it clear that the morning watch is not only a duty, but an unspeakable privilege and pleasure. Fellowship with God, abiding in Christ, loving the Word and meditating on it all the day—to the new nature these things are life and strength, health and gladness. Look upon them in this light; believe in the power of the new nature within, and act upon it; though you do not feel it, it will come true. Count it a joy, and it will become a joy to you.

Above all, realise that the world is needing you and depending on you to be its light. Christ is waiting for you as a member of His body, day by day, to do His saving work through you. Neither he, nor the world, nor you, can afford to lose a single day. God has created and redeemed you, that through you He may, as unceasingly as through the sun He lightens the world, let His light and life and love shine out upon men. You need every day anew to be in communication with the fountain of all light. Do not think of asking for a holiday relief from this intercourse. Still less TAKE it. Prize the holiday for the special time it gives you to study what lay outside your ordinary Bible study course. Prize your holiday for the special opportunity of more fellowship with the Father and the Son. Instead of its becoming a snare, instead of all your energy being exhausted in just being kept from losing ground, prize the holiday as a blessed time for grace and victory over self and the world, of great increase of grace and strength, of being blessed and made a blessing.

XXV

THE INWARD AND THE OUTWARD

"Ye fools, did not He that made that which is without make that which is within also."—LUKE xi. 40.

EVERY spirit seeks to create for itself a form or shape in which its life is embodied. The outward is the visible expression of the hidden inward life. The outward is generally known before the inward; through it the inward is developed and reaches its full perfection, as the apostle says in 1 Cor. xv. 46. "Howbeit that is not first which is spiritual but which is natural, then that which is spiritual." To understand and maintain the right relation between the inward and the outward is one of the greatest secrets of the Christian life.

If Adam in paradise had not listened to the tempter, his trial would have resulted in the perfecting of his inward life. It was his sin and his ruin, and the cause of all his misery, that he gave himself up to the power of the visible outward world. Instead of seeking his happiness in the hidden inward life of a heart in which God's command was honoured, in the inward dispositions of love and faith, of obedience and dependence, he fixed his desire on the world without him, on the pleasure and the knowledge of good and evil that it could give him.

All false religion, from the most degrading idolatry to the corruption of Judaism and Christianity, has its root in this, that what is outward, what can please the eye, or interest the mind, or gratify the taste, takes the place of that truth in the inward part, that hidden wisdom in the heart and life which God seeks and gives.

The great mark of the New Testament is that it is a dispensation of the inner life. The promise of the new covenant is: "I will put My law IN THEIR INWARD PARTS and IN THEIR HEARTS will I write it." "A new heart also will I give you and a new spirit will I put WITHIN YOU and I will put my Spirit WITHIN YOU." The promise of our Lord Jesus was "The Spirit of truth SHALL BE IN YOU. In that day ye shall know that I AM IN YOU." It is in the state of heart that religion consists, in a heart into which God hath sent forth the Spirit of His Son, a heart in which the love of God is shed abroad, that true salvation is found. The inner chamber, with its secret intercourse with the Father, who seeth in secret, is the symbol and the training school of the inner life. The true and faithful daily use of the inner chamber will make the inner hidden life strong and glad.

In all our religion the great danger is giving more time and interest to the outward means than the inward reality. It is not the intensity of your

Bible study, it is not the frequency or the fervency of your prayers or good works, that necessarily constitutes a true spiritual life. No! what we need is, to realise that, as God is a Spirit, so there is a spirit within us that can know and receive Him and become conformed to His likeness, and be partaker of the very dispositions that animate Him as God in His goodness and love.

"Firmly settle this in thy mind, that all our salvation consists in the manifestation of the nature, life and spirit of Christ Jesus in our outward and inward new man. This alone renews and regains the first life of God in the soul of man. Wherever thou goest, whatever thou doest, at home or abroad in the field, do all in a desire of union with Christ, in imitation of His tempers and inclinations, and long for nothing, desire nothing so much, as that which exercises and increases the spirit and life of Christ in thy soul, and to have all within thee changed into the temper and spirit of the holy Jesus.

Consider the treasure thou hast within thee, the Saviour of the world, the eternal Word of God, hid in thy heart as a seed of the Divine Nature which is to overcome sin and death within thee, and generate the life of heaven again in thy soul.

Turn to thy heart, and thy heart will find its Saviour, its God, within itself. Thou seest and feelest nothing of God, because thou seekest for Him abroad, in books, in the church, in outward exercises; but there thou wilt not find Him till thou hast first found Him in thy heart. Seek for Him in thy heart and thou wilt never seek in vain, for there He dwells, there is the seat of His light and Holy Spirit!"

XXVI

THE DAILY RENEWAL—ITS POWER

"Though our outward man perish, yet the inward man is renewed day by day."—2 COR. iv. 16.

"According to His mercy He saved us by the washing of regeneration, and renewing of the Holy Ghost."—1 TIT. iii. 5.

WITH every new day the life of nature is renewed. As the sun rises again with its light and warmth, the flowers open, and the birds sing, and life is everywhere stirred and strengthened. As we rise from the rest of sleep and partake of our morning food, we feel that we have gathered new strength for the duties of the day. The inner chamber is the standing confession of THE NEED OUR INWARD LIFE HAS OF DAILY RENEWAL TOO. It is only by fresh nourishment from God's Word, and fresh intercourse with God Himself in prayer, that the vigour of the spiritual life can be maintained and grow. Though our outward man perish, though the burden of sickness or suffering, the strain of work and weariness may exhaust or enfeeble us, the inward man can be renewed day by day.

A quiet time and place, with the Word and prayer, are the means of the renewal. But only this when as means they are animated by the divine power which works through them. That power is

—the Holy Spirit, the mighty power of God that worketh in us. Our study of the inner chamber and the inner life it represents, would be defective if we did not give its due place to the daily renewal of the inward man, which it is the function of the blessed Spirit ever to work. In the text from Titus we are taught that we have been "saved by the washing of regeneration AND RENEWING OF THE HOLY GHOST." The two expressions are not meant to be a repetition. The regeneration is one great act, the beginning of the Christian life; the renewing of the Holy Ghost is a work that is carried on continuously and never ends. In Romans xii. 2 we read of the progressive transformation of the Christian life, that it is by "THE RENEWING OF THE MIND." In Ephesians iv. 23, while the word "put off the old man" (in the aorist) indicates an act done once for all, the word, "BE RENEWED IN THE SPIRIT OF YOUR MIND" is in the present tense, and points to a progressive work. Even so in Colossians iii. 10 we read, "ye have put on the new man, which is renewed [not, has been] in the image of Him that created him." It is the blessed Spirit to whom we are to look, on whom we can count, for the daily renewal of the inner man in the inner chamber.

Everything depends, in our secret devotions, upon our maintaining the true relation to the adorable third person of the blessed Trinity, through Whom alone the Father and the Son can do their work of saving love, through Whom alone the Christian can do his work. That relation may be expressed in the two very simple words, faith and surrender.

Faith. Scripture says, "God hath sent forth the Spirit of His Son into your hearts, crying, Abba, Father." The child of God, the very feeblest, who would in his morning devotion offer up prayer, that shall be pleasing to the Father, and be a blessing to himself, must remember that he has received the Holy Spirit as the spirit of prayer, and that His help is indispensable to enable us to pray éffectually. Even so with the Word of God. It is by the Holy Spirit alone that the truth in its divine meaning and power can be revealed to us, and do its work in our heart. If the daily renewal of the inward man in the morning hour is to be a reality, take time to meditate, and to worship, and to believe with your whole heart that the Holy Spirit has been given you, that He is within you, and that through Him God will work the blessing which He gives through prayer and the Word.

Surrender. Do not forget that the Holy Spirit must have entire control. "As many as are LED BY THE SPIRIT of God they are the sons of God. They WALK AFTER THE SPIRIT, not after the flesh." It is the ungrieved presence of the Spirit that can give the Word its light and power, and keep us in that blessed life of child-like confidence and child-like obedience which is well pleasing to God. Let us praise God for this wonderful gift, the Holy Spirit in His renewing power, and let us look with new joy and hope to the inner chamber as the place where the inner man can indeed be renewed from day to day. So shall life be kept ever fresh; so shall we go on from strength to strength, so shall we bear much fruit, that the Father may be glorified.

If all this be true, what need that we know the Holy Spirit aright. As the Third Person, it is His office and work to bring the life of God unto us, to hide Himself in the depth of our being and make Himself one with us, to reveal there the Father and the Son, to be the mighty Power of God working in us, and to take control of our entire being. He asks but one thing,—simple obedience to His leading. The truly yielded soul will find in the daily renewing of the Holy Ghost the secret of growth and strength and joy.

XXVII

THE DAILY RENEWAL—THE PATTERN

"Seeing that ye have . . . put on the new man, which is being renewed unto knowledge after the image of Him that created him."—COL. iii. 9, 10.

"If so be that ye heard Him and were taught in Him . . . that ye be renewed in the spirit of your mind, and put on the new man, which after God hath been created in righteousness and holiness of truth."—EPH. iv. 21, 23, 24.

IN every pursuit it is of consequence to have the goal clearly defined. It is not enough that there be movement and progress, we want to know whether the movement be in the right direction, straight for the mark; and especially when we are acting in partnership with another, on whom we are dependent, do we need to know that our aim and his are in perfect accord. If our daily renewal is to attain its object we need to know clearly, and hold firmly to what its purpose is.

"Ye have put on the new man, which is being renewed unto knowledge." The Divine life, the work of the Holy Spirit within us, is no blind force, as in nature. We are to be workers together with God; our co-operation is to be intelligent and voluntary, "The new man is being renewed day by day UNTO KNOWLEDGE." There is a knowledge which the natural understanding can draw from the Word, but which is without life and the power, the real truth and substance, which the spiritual knowledge brings. It is the renewing of the Holy Ghost that gives the true knowledge, which does not consist in thought and conception, but in an inward tasting, a living reception of the very things themselves of which the words and thoughts are but the images. "The new man is being renewed unto knowledge." However diligent our Bible study may be, there is no true knowledge gained any farther than the spiritual renewal is being experienced; "the renewal in the spirit of the mind," in its life and inward being, alone brings true Divine knowledge.

And what is now the pattern that will be revealed to this spiritual knowledge which comes out of the renewal as its true and only aim? The new man is being renewed unto knowledge, AFTER THE IMAGE OF HIM THAT CREATED HIM Nothing less than the image, the likeness of God. That is the one aim of the Holy Spirit in His daily renewing; that must be the aim of the believer who seeks that renewing.

This was God's purpose in creation, "Let us make man in our image, after our likeness." How little the infinite glory of these words is considered. For nothing less than this, did God breathe His own life into man, that it might reproduce in man on earth a perfect likeness to God in heaven. In Christ, that image of God has been revealed and seen in human form. We have been predestined and redeemed and called, we are being taught and fitted by the Holy Spirit, to be conformed to the image of the Son, to be imitators of God, and to walk even as Christ walked. How can the daily renewal be carried on, what can the daily Bible study and prayer profit, unless we set our heart on what God has set His on,—THE NEW MAN BEING RENEWED DAY BY DAY AFTER THE IMAGE OF HIM THAT CREATED HIM.

In the second passage, we have the same thought expressed somewhat differently. Be renewed in the spirit of your mind, and put on the new man, which AFTER GOD, according to the likeness of God, hath been created in righteousness and holiness of truth. Righteousness is God's hatred of sin, and maintenance of the right. Holiness is God's ineffable glory, in the perfect harmony of His righteousness and love, His infinite exaltation above the creature, His perfect union with him. Righteousness in man includes all God's will for our duty to Him or our fellowmen: holiness our personal relation to Himself. As the new man has been created, so it has daily to be renewed, "after God in righteousness and holiness of truth." It is to secure this that the power of the Holy Ghost is working in us. It is to secure this that He waits for us day by day to yield ourselves to Him, in His renewing grace and power.

The daily returning morning hour is the time for securing the daily renewing of the Holy Ghost into the image of God as righteousness and holiness of truth. What need of meditation and prayer to get the heart set upon what God is aiming at, and get a true vision of the wondrous possibility: the inward man renewed day by day into the very likeness of God, changed into the same image as by the Spirit of the Lord. Christian student! let nothing less be thy aim, or satisfy thine aspirations. The image of God, the life of God is in thee, His likeness can be seen in thee. Separate no longer God and His likeness, let everyone approach to Him, let all trust in Him, mean nothing less than finding Him, in His likeness wrought into thee by the renewing of the Holy Spirit.

Let this be thy daily prayer, to be renewed after the image of Him who created thee.

CHAPTER XXVIII

THE DAILY RENEWAL—ITS COST

"Wherefore we faint not; but though our outward man is decaying, yet our inward man is renewed day by day."—2 COR. iv. 16.

"Be not fashioned according to this world; but be ye transformed by the renewing of your mind."—ROM. xii. 2.

IT is not a little or an easy thing to be a full-grown, strong Christian. On God's side, it means that it cost the Son of God His life, that it needs the mighty power of God to new create a man, and that nothing less than the unceasing daily care of the Holy Spirit can maintain that life.

From man's side it demands that when the new man is put on, the old man be put off. All the dispositions, habits, pleasures, of our own nature, that make up the life in which we have lived, are to be put away. All we have by our birth from Adam, is to be sold, if we are to possess the pearl of great price. If a man is to come after Christ, he is to deny himself, and take up his cross, to forsake all and follow Christ in the path in which He walked. He is to cast away not only all sin, but everything, however needful and legitimate and precious, that may become the occasion of sin; to pluck out the eye, or cut off the hand. He is to hate his own life, to lose it, if he is to live in "the power of an endless life." It is a solemn thing, far more solemn than most people think, to be a true Christian.

This is specially true of the daily renewing of the inward man. Paul speaks of it as being accompanied and conditioned by the decaying of the outward man. The whole epistle (2 Cor.) shows us how the fellowship of the sufferings of Christ, even to conformity to His death, was the secret of his life in power and blessing to the Churches. "Always bearing about in the body the dying of Jesus, that the life also of Jesus may be manifested in our body. For we which live are always delivered unto death for Jesus' sake, that the life also of Jesus may be manifested in our mortal flesh. So then death worketh in us, but life in you." The full experience of the life in Christ in our person, our body, our work for others, depends upon our fellowship in His suffering and death. There can be no large measure of the renewal of the inward man, without the sacrifice, the decaying of the outward.

To be filled with heaven, the life must be emptied of earth. We have the same truth in our second text, "Be ye transformed in the renewing of your mind." An old house may be renewed, and yet keep very much of its old appearance; or the renewal may be so entire that men exclaim what a transformation! The renewing of the mind by the Holy Spirit means an entire transformation, an entirely different way of thinking, judging, deciding. The fleshly mind gives place to a "spiritual understanding" (Col. i. 9; 1 John v. 20). This transformation is not obtained but at the cost of giving up all that is of nature. "Be not fashioned according to this world, but be ye transformed." By nature we are of this world. When renewed by grace we are still in the world, subject to the subtle all-pervading influence from which we cannot withdraw ourselves. And what is more, the world is still in us, as the leaven of the nature which nothing can purge out but the mighty power of the Holy Spirit, filling us with the life of heaven.

Let us allow these truths to take deep hold and master us. The Divine transformation, by the daily renewing of our mind into the image of Him who is far above, can proceed in us no faster and no farther than our seeking to be freed from every vestige of conformity to this world. The negative, "Be not fashioned according to this world," needs to be emphasised as strongly as the positive, "be ye transformed." The spirit of this world and the Spirit of God contend for the possession of our being. Only as the former is known and renounced and cast out, can the heavenly Spirit enter in, and do His blessed work of renewing and transforming. The whole world and whatever is of the wordly spirit, must be given up. The whole life and whatever is of self must be lost. This daily renewal of the inward man costs much, that is, as long as we are hesitating, or trying to do it in our own strength. When once we really learn that the Holy Spirit does all, and in the faith of the strength of the Lord Jesus have given up all, the renewing becomes the simple, natural, healthy, joyous growth of the heavenly life in us.

The inner chamber then becomes the place for which we long daily, to praise God for what He has done, and is doing, and what we know He will do. Day by day, we yield ourselves afresh to the blessed Lord who has said, "He that believeth on Me out of him shall flow rivers of living water." "The renewing of the Holy Ghost" becomes one of the most blessed verities of our daily Christian life.

XXIX

HOLINESS—THE CHIEF AIM OF BIBLE STUDY

"Sanctify them in Thy truth, Thy Word is Truth."

IN his great intercessory prayer our Lord spoke of the words which the Father had given Him, of His own giving them to His disciples, and of their having received and believed them. It was this that made them disciples. It was their keeping these words that would really enable them to live the life and do the work of true disciples. RECEIVING THE WORDS OF GOD FROM CHRIST AND KEEPING THEM, THE MARK AND POWER OF TRUE DISCIPLESHIP.

In praying the Father to keep them in the world when he had left it, our Lord asks that He would sanctify them in the truth, as it dwells and works in His word. Christ had said of Himself, "I am the truth." He was the only begotten of the Father, full of grace and truth. His teaching was not like that of the law which came by Moses, giving a knowledge, a promise of good things to come which was but an image or a shadow. "The words I speak unto you are spirit and life," giving the very substance and power and Divine possession of what they speak of. Christ had spoken of the Spirit as the Spirit of truth who would lead into all the truth that there was in Himself, not as a matter of knowledge or doctrine, but into its actual experience and enjoyment. And then He prays that in this living truth, as it dwells in the Word, and is revealed in Him by the Spirit, and the Father would sanctify them. "For their sakes," He says, "I sanctify Myself that they themselves may also be sanctified in truth." And He asks the Father in His power and love to take charge of them, that His object—to sanctify them in the truth, through His word which is truth—may be realised, that they, like Himself, may be sanctified in truth. Let us study the wonderful lessons here given in regard to God's word.

"Sanctify them in Thy truth, Thy word is truth." THE GREAT OBJECT OF GOD'S WORD IS TO MAKE US HOLY. No diligence or success in Bible study will really profit us unless it makes us humbler, holier men. In all our use of Holy Scripture this must be definitely our main object. The reason there is often so much Bible reading with so little real result in a Christ-like character, is that "salvation, through sanctification of the Spirit and belief of the truth," is not truly sought. People imagine that if they study the Word and accept its truths, this will in some way, of itself, benefit them. But experience teaches that it does not. The fruit of holy character, of consecrated life, of power to bless others, does not come, for the simple and most natural reason that we only get what we seek. Christ gave us God's Word to make us holy, it is only when we make this our definite aim in all Bible study, that the truth, not the doctrinal truth, but its Divine quickening power, imparting the very life of God, that it contains as a seed, can open and impart itself to us.

"Sanctify them in Thy truth, Thy word is truth." It is GOD HIMSELF WHO ALONE CAN MAKE US HOLY BY HIS WORD. The word, separate from God and His direct operation, cannot avail. The word is an instrument: God Himself must use it. God is the alone Holy One. He alone can make holy. The unspeakable value of God's word is that it is God's means of holiness. The terrible mistake of many is that they forget that God alone can use it or make it effectual. It is not enough that I have access to the dispensary of a physician. I need him to prescribe. Without him my use of his medicines might be fatal. It was so with the scribes. They made their boast of God's law; they delighted in their study of Scripture and yet remained unsanctified. The word did not sanctify them, because they did not seek for this in the word, and did not yield to God to do it for them.

"Sanctify them in Thy truth, Thy word is truth." THIS HOLINESS THROUGH THE WORD MUST BE SOUGHT AND WAITED FOR FROM GOD IN PRAYER. Our Lord not only taught His disciples that they must be holy; He not only sanctified

Himself for them, that they might be sanctified in truth, but He brought His words and His work to the Father with the PRAYER THAT HE WOULD SANCTIFY THEM. It is most needful to know God's word and meditate on it. It is most needful to set our heart upon being holy, as our first and chief object in studying the Word. But all this is not enough; everything depends upon our following Christ in asking the Father to sanctify us through the Word. IT IS GOD, THE HOLY FATHER, WHO MAKES US HOLY, by the Spirit of holiness who dwells in us. He works in us the very mind and disposition of Christ who is our sanctification. "There is none holy but the Lord"; all holiness is His and what He gives by His holy Presence. The tabernacle and temple were not holy in virtue of cleansing, or separation or consecration. They became holy by the incoming and indwelling God. His taking possession made them holy. God even so makes us holy through His word bringing Christ and the Holy Spirit into us. And the Father cannot do this except as we tarry before Him, and are still, and in deep dependence and full surrender give ourselves up to Him. It is in the prayer offered in the Name, and the fellowship, and the faith of the Great Intercessor— "Sanctify me through Thy truth, Thy word is truth," that the Father's sanctifying power will be found, and our knowledge of God's word truly make us holy.

How sacred the Morning Watch! The hour specially devoted to the Soul's yielding itself up to God's holiness, to be sanctified through the Word. Let us ever remember, the one aim of God's word is to make us holy. Let it be our continual prayer "Father, sanctify me in Thy truth."

XXX

PSALM CXIX AND ITS TEACHING

"Oh how love I Thy law; it is my meditation all the day. Consider how I love Thy precepts. Yea, I love them exceedingly."

In Holy Scripture there is one portion wholly devoted to teaching us the place which God's Word ought to have in our esteem, and the way we can secure its blessing. It is the longest chapter in the Bible, and, with hardly an exception, in every one of its 176 verses, we have, under different names, mention made of the Word. Anyone who really wants to know how to study his Bible according to God's will, ought to make a careful study of this Psalm. There ought to come a time in his life when he resolves to study its teaching and carry it out into practice. How can we wonder that our Bible study does not bring more spiritual profit and strength, if we neglect the Divine Directory it offers us for that study. It is possible you have never read it once through as a whole. If you have not time, find time, some free Sabbath hour—or why not some free week day hour?—in which you read it through and try to take in its chief thought, or at least to catch its spirit. If you find it difficult to do this by reading it once, read it more than once. This will make you feel the need of giving it more careful thought. The following hints may help you in its study:—

1st. Note all the different names under which God's Word is spoken of.

2nd. Note all the different verbs expressing what we ought to feel and do in regard to the Word. Let this lead you to consider carefully what the place is that God's word claims in your heart and life, and how every faculty of your being—desire, love, joy, trust, obedience, action is called out by it.

3rd. Count and note how many times the writer speaks in the past tense of his having kept, observed, stuck to, delighted in God's testimonies. How many times he expresses in the present tense how he rejoices in, loves, and esteems God's law. And then how, in the future tense, he promises and vows to observe God's precepts to the end. Put all these together and see how more than a hundred times he presents his soul before God as one who honours and keeps His law. Study this especially as these expressions are connected with his prayers to God, until you have a clear image of the righteous man whose fervent, effectual prayer availeth much.

4th. Study then the prayers themselves and note down the different requests he makes with regard to the Word, whether for the teaching to understand and the power to observe it, or for the blessing promised in the Word, and to be found in doing it. Note especially prayers like "Teach me Thy statutes," "Give me understanding." Also those where the plea is "according to Thy Word."

5th. Count the verses in which there is any allusion to affliction, whether from his own state or from his enemies, or the sins of the wicked or God delaying "to help him"; and learn how it is in the time of trouble that we need God's Word specially, and that this alone can bring comfort to us.

6th. Then comes one of the most important things. Mark how often the little pronoun Thou, Thine, Thee, occurs, and how often it is understood in every petition, "Teach Thou me," "Quicken Thou me," and you will see how the whole psalm is a prayer spoken to God. All the Psalmist has to say about the Word of God, whether with regard to his own attachment to it, or his need of God's teaching and quickening, is spoken upwards into the face of God. He believes that it is pleasing to God and good for his own soul, to connect his meditation and thoughts on the Word, as continually and as closely as possible, by prayer, with the living God Himself. Every thought of God's Word, instead of drawing him off from God, leads him to fellowship with God.

The word of God becomes to him the rich and inexhaustible material for holding communion with the God Whose it is and to Whom it is meant to lead. As we gradually get an insight into these truths we shall get a new meaning from the single verses. And when, from time to time, we take a whole paragraph with its eight verses, we shall find how they help to lift us up, with and through the word, into God's presence, and into that life of obedience and joy which says, "I have sworn, and will perform it, that I will keep Thy righteous judgment." "Oh how I love Thy law; it is my meditation all the day."

Let us seek by the grace of the Holy Spirit to have the devotional life, which this Psalm reveals, wrought into our morning watch. LET GOD'S WORD every day, and before everything else, LEAD US TO GOD. Let every blessing in it be a matter of prayer, very specially our need of Divine teaching. Let our intense attachment to it be our childlike plea and confidence that the Father will help us. Let our prayers be followed by the vow that as God quickens and blesses us, we shall run the way of His commandments, and let all that God's word brings ourselves make us the more earnest in longing to carry that Word to others, whether for the awakening or the strengthening of the life of God in the soul.

XXXI

THE HOLY TRINITY

"For this cause I bow my knees to THE FATHER that He would grant you, that ye may be strengthened with power THROUGH HIS SPIRIT in the inward man; that CHRIST may dwell in your hearts through faith, to the end that ye, being rooted and grounded IN LOVE, may be strong to know the love of CHRIST which passeth knowledge, that ye may be filled unto all the FULNESS OF GOD. Now unto HIM THAT IS ABLE to do exceeding abundantly above all that we ask or think, according to THE POWER THAT WORKETH IN US, (the Holy Spirit), unto Him be the glory IN CHRIST JESUS for ever and ever. Amen."—EPH. iii. 14-21.

THESE words have often, and not without good reason, been regarded as one of the highest expressions of what the life of a believer may be on earth. And yet this view is not without its dangers, if it fosters the idea that the attainment of such an experience is to be regarded as something exceptional and distant, and hides the blessed truth that, though in varying degree, it yet is meant to be the certain and immediate heritage of every child of God. Each morning each believer has as much the right as the need to say: My Father will strengthen me to-day with power, is strengthening me even now, in the inner man through His Spirit. Each day we are to be content with nothing less than the indwelling of Christ by faith, a life rooted in love, and made strong to know the love of Christ. Each day we believe that the blessed work of being filled in with all the fulness of God is being prepared and carried on and accomplished in us. And each day we ought to be strong in the faith of God's power, and be giving Him glory in Christ, as able to do above what we ask and think, according to the power of the Spirit working in us.

The words are, among many other things, remarkable for the way in which they present the truth of the Holy Trinity in its bearing on our practical life. Many Christians understand that it is right and needful at different times in the pursuit of the Christian life, to give special attention to the three Persons of the Blessed Trinity. They often feel it difficult to combine the various truths into one, and to know how to worship the Three in One. Our text reveals the wondrous relationship and the perfect unity. We have the Spirit within us as the power of God, and yet He does not work at our will or His own. It is the Father who, according to the riches of His glory, grants us to be strengthened "through the Spirit in the inner man." It is the Father who does exceeding abundantly above what we ask or think "according to the Power that worketh in us." So far from the presence of the Spirit within us being to us instead of God, He renders us more absolutely and unceasingly dependent on the

Father. The Spirit can only work as the Father works through Him. We need to combine the two truths—a deep reverent, trustful consciousness of the Holy Spirit as indwelling, with a continual and dependent waiting on the Father to work through Him.

Even so with Christ. We bow our knees to God as Father in the name of the Son. We ask Him to strengthen us through the Spirit with the one object, that Christ may dwell in our heart. So the Son leads to the Father and the Father again reveals the Son in us. And then, again, as the Son dwells in the heart, and it is rooted and grounded in love, drawing its life out of Divine love as its soil, bringing forth fruits and doing works of love, we are led on to be filled with all the fulness of God. The whole heart with the inner and outer life becomes the scene of the blessed interchange of the operation of the Holy Three. As our hearts believe this we give glory through Christ to Him who is able to do more than we can think by His Holy Spirit.

What a wonderful salvation this of which our heart is the scene; the Father ever breathing His Spirit into us, and by His daily renewing fitting it to be the home of Christ; the Holy Spirit ever revealing and forming Christ within us, so that His very nature, disposition, and character becomes ours; the Son imparting His life of love, and leading us on to be filled with all the fulness of God.

This is meant to be our everyday religion. Oh! let us worship the Three-One God in the fulness of faith every day. In whatever direction our Bible study and our prayer lead us, let this ever be the centre from which we go out and to which we return. We were created in the image of the Three-One God. The salvation by which God restores us is an inward salvation; it is nothing to us if it is not wrought in our heart and enjoyed there. The God who saves us can do it in no other way than as the indwelling God, filling us with all His fulness. Let us worship and wait; let us believe and give Him glory.

Have you ever noticed in Ephesians how the three Persons of the Trinity are ever mentioned together.

i. 3. The Father, Jesus Christ, spiritual or Holy Ghost blessings.

i. 12, 13. The Father, to the praise of His Glory, in Christ, sealed with the Holy Spirit.

i. 17. The Father, Our Lord Jesus, the Spirit of Wisdom.

ii. 18. Access through Christ, in one Spirit, to the Father.

ii. 22. In Christ, a habitation of God, through the Spirit.

iii. 4-9. The mystery of Christ, hid in God, preached by the Grace of God, revealed by the Spirit.

iv. 4-6. One Spirit, One Lord, One God and Father.

v. 18-20. Filled with the Spirit, giving thanks to God, in the name of Christ.

vi. 10-18. Strong in the Lord, the whole armour of God, the sword of the Spirit, praying in the Spirit.

As you study and compare these passages, and seek to gather up their teaching in some true and humble conception of the glory of our God, notice specially what an intensely practical truth this of the Holy Trinity is. Scripture teaches little of its mystery in the Divine nature, almost all it has to say has reference to God's work in us, and our faith and experience of His salvation.

A true faith in the Trinity will make us strong, bright, God-possessed Christians. The Divine Spirit making Himself one with our life and inner being; the Blessed Son dwelling in us, as the way to perfect fellowship with God; the Father, through the Spirit and the Son working out day by day His purpose—that we be filled with all the fulness of God.

Let us bow our knees unto the Father! Then the mystery of the Trinity will be known and experienced.

XXXII

IN CHRIST

"Abide in me, and I in you."—John xv. 4.

All instruction proceeds from the outward to the inward.

When some knowledge has been obtained of the actual, in words or deeds, in nature or history, the mind is prepared to seek for the inner meaning hidden in them. It is even so with the teaching of scripture concerning Jesus Christ. He is set before us as a man among us, before us, above us, doing a work for us here on earth, continuing that work for us still in heaven. Many Christians never advance beyond this, an external exalted Lord, in whom they trust for what He has done and is doing for them and in them. They know and enjoy but little of the power of the true mystery of Christ in us, of His inward presence, as an indwelling Saviour.

The former and simpler view is that of the first three Gospels; the latter marks the Gospel of St. John. The former is the aspect of truth presented in the Scripture doctrine of justification. The latter is the teaching concerning the union of the believer with Christ and his continual abiding, as specially taught in St. John and the Epistles to the Ephesians and Colossians.

To the Christians for whom this book is written and who all ought to be preparing to carry Christ to their fellowmen, I cannot say too earnestly: See that this abiding in Christ and Christ in you be not only a truth you hold in its right place in your scheme of Gospel doctrine, but that, as a matter of life and experience, it animate all your faith in Christ and intercourse with God. To be in a room means to have all that there is in it at your disposal, its furniture, its comforts, its light, its air, its shelter. To be in Christ, to abide in Christ, oh! to know what this means. It is not a matter of intellectual faith or conception, but a spiritual reality.

Think who and what Christ is. Consider Him in the five states or stages that mark and reveal His nature and work. He is THE INCARNATE ONE, in whom we see how God's Omnipotence united perfectly the Divine and human nature. Living IN HIM we are partaking of the Divine nature, and of eternal life. He is THE OBEDIENT ONE, living a life of entire surrender to God and perfect dependence on Him. Living IN HIM our life becomes one of complete subjection to God's will and continual waiting upon His guidance. He is THE CRUCIFIED ONE, who died for sin and to sin that He might take it away. Living IN HIM we are free from its curse and dominion, and we live, like Him, in death to the world and our own will. He is THE RISEN ONE, who lives for evermore. Living IN HIM we share His resurrection power, and walk in newness of life, a life that has triumphed over sin and death. He is THE EXALTED ONE, sitting on the throne and carrying on His work for the salvation of men. Living IN HIM His love possesses us, and we give ourselves to Him to use in winning the world back to God. Being in Christ, abiding in Him, means nothing less than that the soul is placed by God Himself in the midst of this wonderful environment of the life of Christ at once human and Divine, utterly given up to God, in obedience and sacrifice, wholly filled with God in resurrection life and glory. The nature and character of Jesus Christ—His dispositions and affections, His power and glory—these are the elements in which we live, the air we breathe, the life in which our life exists and grows.

The full manifestations of God and His saving love can come in no other way than by indwelling. In virtue of Christ's Divinity and Divine power, He can, just so far as we abide in Him, dwell in us. As far as the heart with its love is given to Him in faith, and the will in active obedience, He comes in and makes abode in us. We can say, because we know:—Christ liveth in me.

And now, to come to our main purpose, if this life, Christ in us and we in Him, is to be our real working-day life, its spirit must be renewed and strengthened in the personal intercourse with God with which we begin the day in the morning watch. Our access to God, our sacrifice to God, our expectation from God, must all be in Christ, in the living fellowship with Him. If ever you feel that you want to get nearer to God, to realise His presence or power, or love, or will, or working, more fully, in one word to have more of God —come to God IN CHRIST. Think of how, as man on earth, He drew nigh to the Father in deep humility and dependence, in full surrender and entire obedience, and come in His spirit and disposition, in union with Him. Seek to take the very place before God that Christ has taken in heaven, that of an accomplished redemption, of a perfect victory, of full entrance to God's glory. Take the very place before God that Christ took on earth on His way to the victory and the glory. Do it in the faith of His indwelling and enabling power in you here on earth; count confidently on your approach being accepted not according to your attainment, but according to the uprightness of your heart's surrender, and the completeness of your acceptance in Christ, and you will be led on in the path in which, Christ living in you and speaking in you, will be truth and power.

XXXIII

HIMSELF ALONE

"When Jesus therefore perceived that they would come and take Him by force to make Him a king, He departed again into a mountain Himself alone."—JOHN vi. 15.

THE Gospels frequently tell us of Christ's going into solitude for prayer. Luke mentions his praying eleven times. Mark tells us in his very first chapter, that after an evening when all the city had been gathered together at the door, and He had healed many, "in the morning rising up a great while before day, He went out, and departed into a solitary place and there prayed." Before He chose His twelve apostles "He went out into a mountain to pray, and continued all night in prayer to God." This thought of complete retirement appears to have deeply impressed the disciples, giving rise to John's use of the significant expression, "He departed into a mountain HIMSELF ALONE," as Matthew also had written, "He went up into a mountain apart to pray, and when the even was come, HE WAS THERE ALONE." The man Christ Jesus felt the need of perfect solitude. Let us humbly seek to find out what this means.

1. HIMSELF ALONE. Entirely by Himself,

alone with Himself. We know how much intercourse with men draws us away from ourselves and exhausts our powers. The man Christ Jesus knew this too, and felt the need of coming to Himself again, of gathering all His powers of renewing the consciousness of what He was and what He needed, of realising fully His high destiny, His human weakness, His entire dependence on the Father.

How much more does the child of God need this. Whether it be amid the distraction of worldly engagements or religious service, whether it be for the maintenance of our own Christian life, or the renewal of our power to influence men for God, there is ever an urgent call to every believer to follow in His Master's steps, and find the place and the time where he can indeed be with himself alone.

2. HIMSELF ALONE, with spiritual realities. It is in the entire withdrawal from contact with the things that are seen and temporal that we are free to yield ourselves fully to the powers of the unseen world, and can allow them to master us. Jesus needed time and quiet ever afresh to realise the power of the kingdom of darkness which He had come to contend with and to conquer, the need of this great world of mankind which He had come to save, the presence and the power of the Father whose will He had come to do. Nothing is more indispensable in Christian service than that a man should at times set himself

to think intensely on the spiritual realities with which as a matter of knowledge he is so familiar, and which yet often exercise so little power on the heart and life. The truths of eternity have an infinite power; they are often so powerless because we do not give them time to reveal themselves. Himself alone—this is the only cure.

3. Himself Alone, with God the Father. It is sometimes said that work is worship, that service is fellowship. If ever there were a man who could dispense with special seasons for solitude and fellowship, it was our blessed Lord. But He could not do His work or maintain His fellowship in full power, without His quiet time. He felt the need as man of bringing all His work, past and future, and putting it before the Father, of renewing His sense of absolute dependence on the Father's power, and absolute confidence in the Father's love, in seasons of special fellowship. When He said: "the Son can do nothing of Himself," "as I hear so I speak," He was but expressing the simple truth of His relation to God; it was this that made His going apart a necessity and an unspeakable joy.

Would God that every servant of His understood and practised this blessed art, and that the Church knew how to train its children into some sense of this high and holy privilege, that every believer may and must have his time when he is indeed—himself alone with God. Oh! the thought to have God all alone to myself, and to know that God has me all alone to Himself.

4. HIMSELF ALONE, with the Word. As man our Lord had to learn God's Word as a child; during the long years of His life in Nazareth, He fed on that Word and made it His own. In His solitude He conferred with the Father on all that that Word spoke of Him, on all the will of God it revealed for Him to do.

In the life of the Christian, it is one of the deepest lessons that he has to learn, that the Word without the living God avails little; that the blessing of the Word comes when it brings us to the living God; that the Word that we get from the mouth of God brings the power to know it and to do it. Let us learn the lesson: personal fellowship with God in secret alone can make the word to be life and power.

5. HIMSELF ALONE, in prayer. What an unspeakable privilege prayer is as it allows a man to lay open his whole life to God, and to ask for His teaching and His strength. Just try for a moment to think what prayer meant to Jesus, what adoring worship, what humble love, what child-like pleading for all He needed. As little as we can conceive of this aright, can we realise what blessedness awaits the man who knows to follow in Christ's steps, and to prove what the utmost is that God can do to one who makes this his chief joy—to be with Him, Himself alone.

HIMSELF ALONE. How deep the words open

up to us the secret of the life of Christ on earth, and of the life that He now lives in us. Of the life that He lives in us by His Holy Spirit, this is one of the most blessed elements, that He reveals and imparts to us all that the Word means —Himself alone.

XXXIV

SOUL-WINNING

"He that winneth souls is wise."—PROV. xi. 30.

IN an article in THE STUDENT MOVEMENT for February, 1901, on "A Spiritual Awakening," by H. W. Oldham, I have found the following sentences:—"In the constitutions of most Students' Christian Unions it is stated that THE CHIEF AIM of the S. C. Union is to lead students to become disciples of Jesus Christ. But if the question be pressed home, 'Are students actually being won from indifference and unbelief to faith in Jesus Christ?' the reply must be that, although in a few instances such is the case, in the majority of Unions it is very doubtful. Some Unions, discouraged by previous failure, have become sceptical as to the possibility of winning men for Christ in circumstances so difficult as their own. They may carry on to some extent TRADITIONAL METHODS OF AGGRESSIVE WORK, but have ceased to expect to do more than strengthen such as already have faith. The Executive of the General College Department have definitely set THE SPIRITUAL AWAKENING OF STUDENTS in the forefront of their policy. If the local Unions will rally round the Executive we may fully expect to see God working in the lives of those round about us. The love that won us can win many It is right to recognise the seriousness of adopting this aim. IT INVOLVES CLOSE COMPANIONSHIP WITH JESUS CHRIST IN HOLY LIVING, IN SELF-SACRIFICE, IN LOVING SERVICE; it requires submission to the correction and control of God's Spirit. . . We must lift the aim of WINNING STUDENTS FOR CHRIST out of the background in our work and PLACE IT FIRST. Our Unions have more than sufficient mechanical workers. They need men and women with definite aims, who will think and pray, and pray and work, until their Union is a fit instrument in God's hand for transforming the lives of students."

In an editorial in the same number, we read with regard to the Day of Prayer, "There are many confessions, and many requests which we shall have to make on the day of prayer; but for ourselves we feel that the most urgent must be prayer for a spiritual awakening. We have been gradually recognising the fact that the most of our Unions ARE NOT WINNING MEN FOR CHRIST, and some have begun to realise with dismay that the fact has caused them very little sorrow. 'It is a misfortune certainly that students have not been won, but—what can we do?' Truly a spiritual awakening is needed; needed in our own hearts. When it comes we shall soon find out what to do. Where is the passionate longing to help men? Where is the urgent prayer for our brother that will not be denied? At the very heart of the whole matter is our lack of interest. It is only what interests us that will influence men. It is only when deep down among the eternal interests of our soul there flames THE PASSIONATE DESIRE TO LEAD MEN TO CHRIST, that we shall meet those who need our help, and who will welcome it. It is only words and deeds which burst from the BURNING PASSION OF DESIRE TO HELP MEN, which find opportunities of influencing lives. For it is only where there is a desire like this, that the Holy Ghost is a fellow-worker with men. And without him we are powerless either to find those who are ready, or having found them, to give them help. Shall we not unitedly ask that A PASSION FOR SOULS may be borne in each of us on the day of prayer?"

To this let me add an extract from an article on "Indian Needs," in the January number of the same paper. The writer (Rev. W. E. S. Holland, formerly Trav. Sec. B. C. C. U.) had spoken of the central purpose in the creation of Mission Colleges being "the personal influence which the teachers would be able to gain over their pupils." He had then said: "Yet I have it on the authority of teachers in four of the largest Indian Mission Colleges that their time is so fully taken up with lecturing that they have neither time nor spirit for personal intercourse with their students. Five or six hours a day, with several more in preparation, in an Indian climate, leave a man exhausted, with neither time nor nervous energy for THAT INTENSEST OF ALL WORK, INDIVIDUAL DEALING WITH A MAN ABOUT HIS SOUL."

He concludes his paper with these words: "40,000 men are wanted, not less, if all India is to hear. Yet one almost shrinks from an appeal for men. Why? Lest men should come to be cumberers of the ground. FOR MISSIONARY WORK IS AFTER ALL, ONLY SOUL-WINNING. And there is nothing to make a man a soul-winner in India WHO HAS NOT BEEN ONE AT HOME. A sense of duty, or of the great need, may BRING a man to India. Nothing can enable him to LIVE year by year a missionary LIFE out here, save such a burning love for Christ AS CONSTRAINS TO SACRIFICE AND A LIFE OF SOUL-WINNING AT HOME."

What thoughts these extracts suggest in regard to the work of soul-winning! That it is the first great requisite in the missionary. That going to a mission field will not necessarily make a man a soul-winner. That it is at home, ere one enters the mission field, that the spirit of self-sacrifice and soul-winning must be got and be exercised. That to train its members in the art of soul-winning is one of the chief aims of the Student Movement, as the practice of it will be the measure of its strength and success. That the danger ever threatens of our lapsing out of this into traditional and mechanical methods. That continual, fervent, united and private prayer ought to be made for more love to souls, and continual, earnest, united and private efforts be put forth in every Students' Union that our companions may be won for Christ.

The great characteristic of the Divine life, whether in God, or in Christ, or in us, is—love seeking to save the lost. Let this be the Christian life we cultivate; a love that finds its blessedness in saving men. This life can be cultivated in no other man than by close personal attachment to Jesus, and daily fellowship with Him as a Friend we love. It is in the inner chamber that this fellowship with the Father and the Son is to be maintained. It is in this specially that the father who seeth us in secret will reward us openly.

XXXV.

THE POWER OF INTERCESSION

"TELL me wherein thy great strength lieth." —It is the question we fain would have answered of the men who of old, and in later times, as intercessors for others, have had power with God, and have prevailed. More than one, who has desired to give himself to this ministry, has wondered that he has found it so difficult to rejoice in it, to persevere, and to prevail. Let us study the lives of the leaders and heroes of the prayer world; maybe some of the elements of their success will be discovered to us.

The true intercessor is a man who knows that God knows of him that his heart and life are WHOLLY GIVEN UP TO GOD AND HIS GLORY. This is the only condition on which an officer at the court of an earthly sovereign could expect to exert much influence. Moses and Elijah and Daniel and Paul prove that it is so in the spiritual world. Our blessed Lord is Himself the proof of it. He did not save us by intercession, but by self-sacrifice. His power of intercession roots in His sacrifice: it claims and receives what the sacrifice won. As we have it so clearly put in the last words of Isaiah liii.: "He poured out His soul unto death, and was numbered with the transgressors, and He bare the sins of many," —study this in connection with the whole chapter of which it is the crown—"and made intercession for the transgressors." He first gave himself up to the will of God. There he won the power to influence and guide that will. He gave Himself for sinners in all-consuming love, and so He won the power to intercede for them. There is no other path for us. It is the man who seeks to enter personally into death with Christ, and gives himself wholly for God and men, who will dare to be bold like Moses or Elijah, who will persevere like Daniel or Paul. Whole-hearted devotion and obedience to God are the first marks of an intercessor.

You complain that you do not feel able to pray thus, and ask how you may be fitted to do so. You speak much of the feebleness of your faith in God, and love to souls, and delight in prayer. The man who is to have power in intercession must cease these complaints—he must know that he has A NATURE PERFECTLY ADAPTED TO THE WORK. An apple tree is only expected to bear apples, because it has the apple nature within it. "You are God's workmanship, created in Christ Jesus unto good works." The eye was created to see: how beautifully fitted it is for its work! You are created in Christ to pray. It is your very nature as a child of God; the Spirit has been sent into your heart—what to do? To cry Abba Father, to draw your heart up in child-like prayer.

The Holy Spirit prays in us with groanings that cannot be uttered, with a divine power which our mind and feelings cannot understand. Learn, if you would be an intercessor, to give the Holy Spirit much greater honors than is generally done. Believe that He is praying within you, and then be strong and of good courage. As you pray, be still before God to believe and yield to this wonderful power of prayer within you.

But there is so much conscious sinfulness and defect in our prayer? True, but have you not learned what it is to pray IN THE NAME OF CHRIST? Does the name not mean the living power? Do you not know that you are in Christ and He in you? That your whole life is hid and bound up in His? and His whole life is hid and working in you? The man who is to intercede in power must be very clear that, not in thought and reckoning only, but in the most actual, living, divine reality, Christ and he are one in the work of intercession. He appears before God clothed with the name and the nature, the righteousness and worthiness, the image and spirit and life of Christ. Do not spend your chief time in prayer in reiterating your petition, but in humbly, quietly, confidently claiming your place in Christ, your perfect union with Him, your access to God in Him. It is the man who comes to God in Christ, bringing to the Father that Christ in whom He delights, as his life and his law and only trust who will have power to intercede.

Intercession is preëminently a work of faith. Not the faith that tries only to believe the prayer will be heard, but the faith that is at home amid heavenly realities. A faith that does not trouble about one's own nothingness and feebleness, because it is living in Christ. A faith that does not make its hope depend upon its feelings, but upon the faithfulness of the Three-One God, in what each person has undertaken to do in prayer. A faith that has overcome the world, and sacrifices the visible to be wholly free for the spiritual and heavenly and eternal to take possession of it. A faith that knows that it is heard and receives what it asks, and therefore quietly and deliberately perseveres in its supplication till the answer come. The true intercessor must be a man of faith.

The intercessor must be a MESSENGER—one who holds himself ready, who earnestly offers himself personally to receive the answer and to dispense it. Praying and working go together. Think of Moses—his boldness in pleading with God for the people was no greater than his pleading with the people for God. We see the same in Elijah—the urgency of his prayer in secret is equalled by his jealousy for God in public, as he witnessed against the sin of the nation. Let intercession be always accompanied, not so much, by more diligent work, as by the meek and humble waiting on God to receive His grace and spirit, and to know more definitely what and how He would have us work. It is one thing, it is a great thing, to begin to take up the work of intercession—the drawing down to earth of the blessings which heaven has for its every need. It is a greater thing as intercessor personally to receive that blessing, and go out from God's face, knowing that we have secured something that we can impart. May God make us all whole-hearted, believing, blessing-bearing intercessors.

XXXVI

THE INTERCESSOR

"The effectual fervent prayer of a righteous man availeth much. Elias was a man subject to like passions as we are."—JAS. v. 16, 17.

THERE is nothing that so much weakens the force of the call to imitate the example of Scripture saints, as the thought that theirs are exceptional cases, and that what we see in them is not to be expected of all. The aim of God in Scripture is the very opposite. He gives us these men for our instruction and encouragement, as a specimen of what His grace can do, as living embodiments of what His will and our nature at once demand and render possible.

It was just to meet the so common error alluded to, and to give confidence to all of us who aim at a life of effectual prayer, that James wrote: "Elias was a man subject to like passions as we are." As there was no difference between his nature and ours, or between the grace that wrought in him and works in us, there is no reason why we should not, like him, pray effectually. If our Prayer is to have power, we must seek to have somewhat of Elijah's spirit. The aspiration, Let me seek grace to pray like Elijah, is perfectly legitimate, is most needful. If we honestly seek for the secret of his power in prayer the path in which he trod will open to us. We shall find it in his life with God, his work for God, his trust in God.

Elijah Lived with God.

Prayer is the voice of our life. As a man lives so he prays. Not the words or thoughts with which he is occupied at set times of prayer, but the bent of his heart as seen in his desires and actions, .is regarded by God as his real prayer. The life speaks louder and truer than the lips. To pray well I must live well. He who seeks to live with God, will learn so to know His mind and to please Him, that he will be able to pray according to His will. Think how Elijah, at his first message to Ahab, spoke of "the Lord God, before whom I stand." Think of his solitude at the brook Cherith, receiving his bread from God through the ravens, and then at Sarepta through the ministry of a poor widow. He walked with God, he learned to know God well; when the time came, he knew how to pray to a God whom he had proved. It is only out of a life of true fellowship with God that the prayer of faith can be born. Let the link between the life and the prayer be clear and close. As we give ourselves to walk with God, we shall learn to pray.

Elijah Worked for God.

He went where God sent him. He did what

God commanded him. He stood up for God and his service. He witnessed against the people and their sin. All who heard him could say: "Now I know that thou art a man of God, and that the word of the Lord in thy mouth is truth." His prayers were all in connection with his work for God. He was equally a man of action and a man of prayer. When he prayed down, first the drought and then the rain, it was, as part of his prophetic work, that the people, by judgment and mercy, might be brought back to God. When he prayed down fire from heaven on the sacrifice, it was that God might be known as the true God. All he asked was for the glory of God. How often believers seek power in prayer, that they may be able to get good gifts for themselves. The secret selfishness robs them of the power and the answer. It is when self is lost in the desire for God's glory, and our life is devoted to work for God, that power to pray can come. God lives to love, and save, and bless men: the believer who gives himself up to God's service in this, will find in it new life in prayer. Work for others proves the honesty of our prayer for them. Work for God reveals alike our need and our right to pray boldly. Cultivate the consciousness, and speak it out before God, that you are wholly given up to His service; it will strengthen your confidence in His hearing you.

Elijah Trusted God.

He had learned to trust Him for His personal

needs in the time of famine; he dared trust Him for greater things in answer to prayer for His people. What confidence in God's hearing him we see in his appeal to the God that answers by fire. What confidence in God's doing what he would ask, when he announced to Ahab the abundance of rain that was coming, and then, with his face to the earth, pleaded for it, while his servant, six times over, brought the message, "There is nothing." An unwavering confidence in the promise and character of God, and God's personal friendship for himself, acquired in personal intercourse, and proved in work for God, gave power for the effectual prayer of the righteous man.

The inner chamber is the place where this has to be learned. The morning watch is the training school where we are to exercise the grace that can fit us to pray like Elijah. Let us not fear. The God of Elijah still lives; the spirit that was in him dwells in us. Let us cease from the limited and selfish views of prayer, which only aim at grace enough to keep us standing. Let us cultivate the consciousness that Elijah had of living wholly for God, and we shall learn to pray like him. Prayer will bring to ourselves and to others the new and blessed experience, that our prayers too are effectual and avail much.

In the power of that Redeeming Intercessor, who ever liveth to pray, let us take courage and not fear. We have given ourselves to God, we are working for Him. We are learning to know and trust Him. We can count on the life of God in us, the Holy Spirit dwelling in us, to lead us on to this grace too: the effectual prayer of the righteous man that availeth much.

A List of

Rev. Andrew Murray's Works

Authorized Editions

PUBLISHED BY

Fleming H. Revell Company

NEW YORK, CHICAGO, TORONTO
LONDON AND EDINBURGH

The Ministry of Intercession.

A Plea for More Prayer. 16mo, cloth, 75c.

A Companion volume to "With Christ in the School of Prayer," and a further elaboration of the same great theme. A valuable appendix, entitled "Pray Without Ceasing: Helps to Intercession," contains prayers for a month, and other aids and guides to the life of prayer.

Pray Without Ceasing.

Per doz., net, 35c; per hundred, net, $2.50.

The appendix to "The Ministry of Intercession."

The Lord's Table.

A Help to the Right Observance of the Holy Supper. Long 16mo, cloth, 50c.

Meditations and Prayers for Communion Sabbath, and for each day of the weeks before and after.

Waiting on God.

Daily Messages for a Month. Long 16mo, cloth, 50c.

"Sets forth very simply and clearly the blessedness of a life in which God is unceasingly giving and working, His child unceasingly waiting and receiving."—*Christian Advocate* (*N. Y.*)

The Children for Christ.

12mo, cloth, $1.00.

"The work is admirable in, and well adapted to, its holy purpose."—*The N. Y. Observer.*

The New Life.

Words of God for Young Disciples of Christ. 12mo, cloth, 50c.

Specially designed for young disciples. Some of the subjects treated are "Faith," "The Power of God's Word," "The Confession of Sin," "Holiness," "Humility," "Personal Work."

The Holiest of All.

An Exposition of the Epistle to the Hebrews. 8vo, cloth, net, $2.00.

In this exposition the author seeks to answer the common questions, What is the want in our religion, that, in so many cases, it gives no power to stand, to advance, to press on unto perfection? And what is the teaching that is needed to give that health and vigor to the Christian life that, through all adverse circumstances, may be able to hold fast the beginning firm to the end?

The Spiritual Life.

12mo, cloth, 50c.

A series of lectures delivered before the students of the Moody Bible Institute, Chicago.